KNOCKING THE HUSTLE

AGAINST THE NEOLIBERAL TURN IN BLACK POLITICS

LESTER K. SPENCE

punctum books brooklyn, n.y.

KNOCKING THE HUSTLE: AGAINST THE
NEOLIBERAL TURN IN BLACK POLITICS
© 2015 Lester K. Spence

Revised edition: April 2016.
First published in 2015 by
punctum books
Brooklyn, New York
http://punctumbooks.com

punctum books is an independent, open-access
publisher dedicated to radically creative modes of
intellectual inquiry and writing across a whimsical
para-humantities assemblage. We solicit and pimp
quixotic, sagely mad engagements with textual
thought-bodies. We provide shelters for intellectual
vagabonds.

ISBN-13: 978–0692540794
ISBN-10: 0692540792

Cover photo: Lester Spence.
Facing-page drawing: Heather Masciandaro.
Book design: Chris Piuma.
Editorial assistance: Bert Fuller and Kristen McCants.

Before you start to read this book,

take this moment to think about making a donation to **punctum books**, an independent non-profit press,

@ http://punctumbooks.com/about/

If you're reading the e-book, you can click on the image below to go directly to our donations site. Any amount, no matter the size, is appreciated and will help us to keep our ship of fools afloat. Contributions from dedicated readers will also help us to keep our commons open and to cultivate new work that can't find a welcoming port elsewhere. Our adventure is not possible without your support.

Vive la open-access.

Fig. 1. Hieronymus Bosch, *Ship of Fools* (1490–1500)

CONTENTS

Dedicated to
LaVita Wright Liverspoon (1969–2014),
to Sam Isbell (1968–2001),
and to the Spence Clan
(Imani, Kamari, Kiserian,
Niara, and Khari)

ACKNOWLEDGMENTS

THANKS TO MY AGENT SHOSHANA CRICHTON FOR HER WORK. Eileen Joy and the staff at punctum for taking the risk. Tamara K. Nopper for her wonderful editing assistance. The Breakfast Club for the semi-daily affirmation. Abigail Breiseth, Denise Lever, Camilla Seiler, Jay Gillen, and David Jonathan Cross, for thoughtful comments (and to Sam Chambers, Bret Gustafson, Clarissa Hayward, Fredrick Harris, Taeku Lee, Tamara Nopper, Rogers Smith, Steve Teles, and Dorian Warren for comments on the SOULS article this comes out of). The Sons of Blood and Thunder for Manhood, Scholarship, Perseverance, and Uplift (Sam Kirkland, Darius McKinney, Glenn B. Eden, Selvan Man-thiram, Lee Rudolph, Kurmell Knox, and Caurnel Morgan in particular). Hanes Walton, Richard Iton, Nick Nelson, and Stu-art Hall (RIP) for providing examples. The Department of Polit-ical Science and the Center for Africana Studies at Johns Hop-kins University for providing a home. The members of Hopkins' noon basketball game for providing a court. My children and family for providing a reason. The Institute for Research in African-American Studies at Columbia University, the Murray Weidenbaum Center at Washington University in St. Louis, and the Political Science Departments at the University of Califor-nia at Berkeley and the University of Pennsylvania for provid-ing a platform. Don Palmer and Beth Frederick, for providing a third space. The Red Emmas Collective, LBS, RAF, the Algebra Project, RTHA, West Wednesdays, Equity Matters, BUC, and the general 313, 248, and 734 area codes (Detroit, Inkster, Ann Arbor, and Southfield in particular) for providing alternatives. Marc Steiner for providing ammunition. And as always a spe-cial thanks to those who antagonistically cooperated with me in writing this book. The errors, of course, are mine.

FOREWORD

IN 1896, PAUL LAURENCE DUNBAR PUBLISHED A POEM TITLED "We Wear the Mask".

> We wear the mask that grins and lies,
> It hides our cheeks and shades our eyes, —
> This debt we pay to human guile;
> With torn and bleeding hearts we smile,
> And mouth with myriad subtleties,
> Why should the world be over-wise,
> In counting all our tears and sighs?
> Nay, let them only see us, while
> We wear the mask.
> We smile, but, O great Christ, our cries
> To thee from tortured souls arise.
> We sing, but oh the clay is vile
> Beneath our feet, and long the mile;
> But let the world dream otherwise,
> We wear the mask!

Dunbar writes of black men and women at the turn of the twentieth century forced to "wear the mask" because of racism.

I've worn a mask, but not that one.

I'm writing this draft a day after I received word that my house has been "saved", with "saved" placed in quotes because I am still in the middle of Bank of America hell. I had gone almost three years without paying—the last check I remember cutting to the bank was in December of 2010 or January 2011. I remember the moment I decided to stop like it was yesterday, just like I remember the moment two men came to my home to repossess my car.

Let me back up a moment.

* * *

October 2006

It was 1:30 AM on a late Saturday night and I was in my office, working. There are probably three aspects of being a professor most people outside of the Academy routinely misunderstand. The first aspect they misunderstand is the role writing and research play in our jobs and in our lives. I wasn't up at 1:30 AM because I was thinking about a lecture, or preparing for class. I was up "club late" because I was writing. Trying to scratch out one more paragraph, one more sentence, one more word. And failing miserably. Relatedly, the second thing they misunderstand is how hard writing can be, even for someone like me — I've been writing in one way or another since I was 3 years old. One of the reasons I decided to pursue a job in the Academy in the first place is because I knew that if I played my cards right I'd be able to write and collect a check doing it. But that doesn't mean it's easy. Particularly under stress.

Which brings me to the third aspect. The Academy is like a multi-tiered economy, with four types of intellectual laborers. At the top are tenured professors, people who have the equivalent of lifetime jobs. Under them are tenure-track professors, people who do *not* have lifetime jobs but have the potential to get them if they work hard. And under *them* are adjunct faculty, who are not tenured and do not even have the potential to be tenured, and live incredibly precarious lives even though in many cases they have PhDs.[1] And then, alongside of them

---

1   The individual story of Margaret Mary Vojtko who passed away Sept. 1, 2013 is particularly important here. She'd spent over 25 years as an adjunct at Duquesne University, teaching French. According to union organizer Daniel Kovalik (2013), Ms. Vojtko was a cancer patient, and after Duquesne cut her salary to $10,000 was no longer able to afford her medical bills and her home. Forced effectively to live out of her office, Duquesne fired her. She died months after.

to a certain extent, are graduate students, people who *want* to become tenure-track professors so they can *become* tenured professors, but given the paucity of tenure-track jobs will have to fight hard not to become adjuncts.

I was on the tenure track, and knew I was hanging by a thread.

So I worked. In this case about 45 minutes too long.

Barely two minutes after I left campus a white Jeep Cherokee smashed into my minivan.

I was ok, but the car wasn't.

The minivan was the only car we had. And it was just about to be paid off. My wife and I didn't have savings for a down payment for another car. We didn't even have enough money to get reimbursed for a car rental. And we had five children to shuttle back and forth.

For a week local friends shuttled us back and forth. I bought a bus pass, and took the bus to work. Because we homeschooled our kids we were part of a large black homeschool network. The parents in this network brought groceries, prepared meals, and helped shuttle our kids around. We were ok for a couple of weeks.

Then my children were involved in another accident.

Every Saturday my family made the trek up to the YMCA. T-ball, soccer, basketball, dance—you name it, our kids did it. Without the minivan we didn't know how this would continue, but one of the homeschool parents came to our aid. She would drive to our house, pick up the kids in her minivan and would take them to the Y.

Not two weeks after my accident, our friend picks up our kids to take them to the Y. Twenty minutes after she leaves we get a phone call.

She was in a car crash. The car flipped over.

Everyone was ok. Given the nature of the accident it was a miracle.

Being hit with these accidents within two weeks of each other was incredibly draining. We needed to get back on sound footing. The first step was finding a vehicle.

One of my fraternity brothers worked at a car dealership. I'd told my brothers what had happened. One of them emailed me and told me that he had a car for me. At first I thought he meant that he had a car for me to *buy*—something I couldn't do because I didn't have the money.

No.

He loaned us a brand new SUV. I didn't have to pay a *dime*. All I had to do was bring it back like I found it.

He wasn't the only one. My father-in-law had a working van that he no longer drove, and he promised it to us. Further, another homeschool parent gave us an older car to drive. Within a few weeks we had three cars to replace the one we'd lost.

* * *

Every now and then I conduct research experiments. Let's conduct one now. Change three details about the story I just told you. Make me a low level Walmart employee with no college degree. Finally, change my parents' financial circumstance.[2]

What happens after that first car crash? I noted that I took the bus to work (the MTA 22 to be exact—the same bus I use to this day). As a professor I only have to be on campus on the days I teach.

The only clock I had was the tenure clock. In other words, I have a relative degree of flexibility.

But what if I worked at Walmart?

If I worked at Walmart, my single twenty-minute bus ride becomes 40 minutes longer, with another bus and a metro trip thrown in for good measure. Which on the surface doesn't appear to be too bad. However, neither the two buses nor the Metro runs exactly on time, so even if I'm at the bus/metro stop on time...the bus/metro might not be.[3] And if even one of the buses or the metro is just a bit off schedule everything else is

---

2   Of course this thought experiment is a bit tricky, because if I worked at Walmart...or didn't have a PhD...or didn't have parents with resources, I wouldn't have been at Hopkins to get in the car accident in the *first* place, right? But bear with me.

3   On more than one occasion I beat the bus home because, rather than wait for it, I decided to walk.

thrown out of whack. The first bus might be on time, and the last bus might be on time, but if the metro isn't on time . . . then I'm out of luck.

Further, working at Walmart isn't the same as working as a tenure-track university professor at a high-tier university. If I'm scheduled to work at Walmart from 9 to 5, I've got to be there at 9. If I come in late, I'd lose pay . . . and likely my job if it happened more than once, even if it wasn't my fault. If I had to rely on public transportation it would likely have cost me my job. And would have put my family at severe risk. I can hear the manager now. "You should have taken the earlier bus."

Being a professor has its own grind but it provides me with flexibility—I work far more than forty hours per week but I work the majority of those hours when and where I want. It also provides me with benefits. Health insurance covered most of the costs associated with the accident. Even if I were somehow able to keep my Walmart job with no car, Walmart's idea of "job benefits" is to have workers covered by Medicaid rather than provide them with health care. How would my story differ if we took away my college education? If I didn't attend college, I wouldn't have access to any of the networks I relied on. I wouldn't be able to rely on my fraternity brothers because I wouldn't be in the fraternity. The vast majority of the parents in the black homeschool network I was a part of were also college educated. So it's unlikely I'd have people in my life with the ability to just *give* me a car.

I thought about all of this as I was in the middle of it, as I was thinking about how I was going to get to work, as I was thinking about how I was going to get another car, as I was thinking about how I was going to pay whatever bills left over from the accident. I realized how blessed I was to be able to emerge from the accident relatively unscathed, how blessed I was to be connected with people who would look out for me. And I realized that if I were different, if my life had gone just a bit differently, I'd be in a very very different place.

Now many would probably say in response that I worked hard to get to where I am, that my parents and my in-laws worked hard to put my family in the position where getting into a car accident isn't a life-changing event. In black (and other) churches around the country, prosperity gospel pastors routinely use the phrase *favor isn't fair* to argue that God's blessings tend to go to God's people. My story, then, can be read as the story of someone who, because of his favor (that is, because of the type of job he had and the networks he had as a result of his education and his upbringing), was able to take a couple of minor setbacks and overcome them. My race and gender here makes the story even better—black man faces setback, emerges triumphant!

But this narrative, told in black communities across the country, ignores a couple of important things. The first thing it ignores is that our ability to bounce back from life's challenges aren't *and should not be* simply dictated by favor . . . by whether we went to the right schools, or by whether or how we believe in God (or the "right" God), or by whether we have the right networks.

We are fooling ourselves if we believe there is something inherent about what we do as people who purport to be middle or upper class that causes us to deserve the benefits we do receive, that "working hard" or "being faithful" or doing one's duty as a brother should automatically confer certain benefits. If favor isn't fair, it *should* be. Everyone should have access to the resources and networks I had access to in that moment, regardless of their employment, regardless of their religious background, regardless of their personal connections. But we routinely make comparisons between the deserving and undeserving. The idea that "favor isn't fair" produces and reproduces crises that do significant damage to black communities.

But the second thing we miss is the unique stresses and strains the contemporary condition causes even for the supposedly favored among for us.

Which brings me back to that mask.

* * *

October 2008

Although I emerged from the accident without a physical scratch I did not emerge from the accident unharmed. It was a while before the insurance claim came through, so we were forced to reply on makeshift transportation options for months. When the claim did come through we had enough money to pay off the old car, but not enough to buy a new car outright—we didn't have savings. Every dollar, every *penny* I brought in, immediately went out. Our car was only several months away from being paid off, and we literally banked on that extra money to provide us with a cushion.

But now, we had to postpone that vision. Instead of having only eight months of car payments we had to now add another 64 months to that. And as our kids were growing older the bills we accumulated grew. We spent more on food. We spent more on clothing. We spent more on utilities.

The next year went by in a blur. Every month we were just a little bit short—one month on rent, another month on heat, another month on the car. Every month it seemed as if we were relying on our network a little bit more for money.

I mentioned the fact that we homeschooled our children.

While we rented in one of the best black neighborhoods in Baltimore, the elementary school was horrible. I remember the day I looked over my oldest daughter's math homework. They were working on decimal points, and on her worksheet she was assigned to state whether various mathematical statements were "true" or "false". For example the mathematical statement $2.4 > 2.0$ is "true" while the mathematical statement $2.1 < 1.9$ is "false". She marked the mathematical statement $1.0 > 1$ "false". The teacher marked the statement wrong, which meant that 1.0 and 1 had different numerical values. So I tell my daughter the teacher is wrong—that 1.0 and 1 have the same value even though the two are written differently. Her response? "But daddy, she's my *teacher*."

After this I look at her homework more closely, noticing a number of words her teacher misspelled on homework assignments. And after our oldest son's second grade teacher told us she wouldn't send her own child to the school we figured the problem wasn't our children but rather the school.

Private school wasn't an option for us because we didn't have the money. So homeschool was the only option we had left. My wife found a black homeschool group in the city, and was able to provide our children with a better education than they would have received if they'd have stayed in that elementary school. But bills continued to pile up.

When our landlord asked us to pay a portion of our energy bill because of skyrocketing energy prices, we realized we needed another income...which meant we needed to move to find a better public school system. Which meant we needed to buy a house.

We scraped up the money through a combination of family and my retirement account, and got enough for a mortgage down payment. Our kids could go to school right around the block. And my wife could begin to look for work.

But this made our circumstances even tighter, because now I had to pay every bill I'd paid before, plus utilities and the loan I'd taken for the down payment on the house.

(Even writing this down makes me want to take a deep breath.)

During all of this I was still expected to work. To be a good teacher. To publish in scholarly journals. To write a book good enough to be published by the best academic presses. To collaborate with colleagues. I mentioned above that being a tenure-track university professor has its own grind.

I went into overdrive.

I would wake up at 4:30 AM, then write for hours. Then go to work. Then try to write some more. Then come home at around 6:30 PM. Eat, talk to my wife and kids for about an hour, then go to bed.

When I woke up I would repeat the process. Write. Work. Come home for a bit. Eat. Sleep. Wake up. Write. Work. Come home. Eat. Sleep. Write. Work. Always feeling as if I were behind, as if there were more work to do, as if I didn't have enough hours in the day, in the week, in the month.

After more than a year, it all caught up with me.

One weekend, the weight of everything that had happened to us up to that point, the car crash, the bills, the decision to move, the homeschooling, the robbing Peter to pay Paul, the lack of savings, the missed mortgage payments, all the (in my mind, bad) choices we'd made, all of it came crashing down.

And I collapsed. And I didn't get out of bed for three days straight.

I hadn't considered medication before. I got a prescription for an anti-depressant. It didn't take our bills away, it didn't miraculously write my book for me. But they enabled me to be a bit more capable of doing what I had to do to survive.

By 2010, two years after America elected the first self-identified black president, the car we bought as a result of the accident had been repossessed, and I was facing foreclosure.

The mask.

Throughout the entire ordeal, I donned the mask, to the extent I could. I didn't miss a class. I didn't miss a writing day. I told very few colleagues. I fulfilled all of my obligations as if I didn't have a care in the world.

* * *

In June 2011 the University of Minnesota Press published *Stare in the Darkness: The Limits of Hip-hop and Black Politics*, the book I was working on before, during, and after the accident. It represented an attempt to subject the various claims scholars, activists, and others have made about hip-hop to critical scrutiny. But it also represented an attempt to understand how black communities reproduce inequality, sometimes through black popular culture.

Even in this supposed post-racial era, a range of writers, activists, and policy-makers examine inter-racial inequality. In fact a growing number of scholars have become interested in *intra-racial* politics, the politics that occurs within racial groups. I've spent most of my life in and around three majority black cities, Detroit, St. Louis, and Baltimore — cities with large black populations. Even as racism still shapes the lives blacks in these cities lead, racism cannot explain why some blacks in these areas have a lot of resources and some have a few. Racism cannot explain why there are some black populations we as black men and women are all too willing to fight for, while there are other black populations we are willing to let die. And racism cannot fully explain how black people choose to fight, nor can it fully explain the solutions black people generate for the problems they face.

What can?

The neoliberal turn, the gradual embrace of the general idea that society (and every institution within it) works best when it works according to the principles of the market, can go part of the way. We now routinely refer to public officials as people we *hired* rather than elected, as CEOs rather than political representatives. We place business executives with more managerial expertise than educational expertise in charge of public school systems. We use the Bible (and increasingly the Koran) as entrepreneurial self-help guides rather than as spiritual texts. We increasingly believe an array of public goods and services (from education to utility provision to social security) are better off distributed by private profit-making actors. Finally, we no longer respect the dignity of labor, and increasingly propose hustling to make ends meet. The neoliberal turn helps explain the rise of inequality, the increasing anxiety and insecurity we all feel (regardless of how much money we make or what type of job we have), how a number of institutions (including but not limited to black churches) we've relied on have been transformed, how narrow our political imaginations have become.

The story I began this with is not a life or death story. But it is a story about a certain type of suffering, a masked suffering, that even when healed is done so problematically, "problematically" because the various ways we (and here I not only refer to African Americans but to Americans in general) tend to heal this suffering are woefully inadequate, in part because we haven't properly identified what causes our suffering in the first place. The crises my family faced are the natural end-products of a society that increasingly shirks its responsibilities to those perceived to be losers in an increasingly stark competition over material, social, and psychic resources.

Over the several chapters to follow I seek to make plain the suffering that black populations, black institutions, and black cities undergo in this contemporary moment. For a variety of reasons we've been forced to hustle and grind our way out of the post-civil rights era, and it is this hustle and grind in all of its institutional manifestations that's resulted in our current condition. While interest in neoliberalism is growing, writings that examine how neoliberalism shapes black life are few and far between. I rectify this gap with an eye towards contributing to the scholarly literature, but more importantly with an eye towards contributing to the broader conversation about solutions.

OVER FIFTY YEARS AGO, JAZZ CORNETIST NAT ADDERLEY recorded "Work Song". Oscar Brown Jr. later added lyrics and included the record on his album *Sin & Soul . . . and Then Some.*

> Breaking rocks out here on the chain gang
> Breaking rocks and serving my time
> Breaking rocks out here on the chain gang
> Because they done convicted me of crime
> Hold it steady right there while I hit it
> Well reckon that ought to get it
> Been working and working
> But I still got so terribly far to go
> (Adderley and Brown Jr. 1961)

For much of the twentieth century black (and some poor white) prisoners were forced to labor for southern businesses in prisons like Mississippi's Parchman Farm (Oshinsky 1996).[1] "Work Song" tells the story of a poor hungry worker convicted for stealing food from a grocery store.

Motown was two years old when "Work Song" was released. Against "Work Song" I put Ace Hood's "Hustle Hard".

> . . . same old shit, just a different day
> Out here tryna get it, each and every way
> Mama need a house, baby need some shoes
> Times are getting hard, guess what I'ma do

---

1 Often imprisoning men for the weakest of infractions, political officials subcontracted prison labor out to business interests, often increasing arrest rates when businesses needed more laborers.

> Hustle, hustle, hustle, hard
> Hustle, hustle, hustle, hard
> Hustle, hustle, hustle, hard
> Closed mouths don't get fed on this boulevard
>   (Hood and Luger 2011)

The hustle. The concept of the "hustler" has changed somewhat over the past thirty years or so. Whereas in the late sixties and early seventies the hustler was someone who consistently sought to get over, the person who tried to do as little work as possible in order to make ends meet, with the "hustled" being the people who were victimized by these individuals ("He *hustled* me"), the hustler is now someone who consistently works. I can't go a week on the subway without seeing someone sell incense or gloves in the winter. I can't wait for the MTA 22 bus at Mondawmin mall for more than ten minutes without running into someone selling "loose ones" (individual cigarettes) or bottled water during the summer. And the hustle, rather than being the act of trying to get over, has now been transformed to the point where it means the exact opposite: "hustle" and "grind" are now often used interchangeably. Much of rap explicitly exalts the daily rise-and-grind mentality black men with no role in the formal economy need to possess in order to survive and thrive. Black Sheep (1994) in his track "Autobiographical" rhymes about selling drugs on the street in sub-zero weather. In Kanye West's "Diamonds from Sierra Leone (remix)" (2005) Jay-Z says "I'm not a businessman, I'm a *business,* man!" These and dozens of other rap records depict MCs as risk-taking street entrepreneurs consistently having to make ends meet, responsible for success/failure. Ace Hood is willing to do whatever he needs to do ("Mama needs a house. Baby needs some shoes. Times are getting hard. Guess what I'ma do?" Sell clothes, bootleg CDs, candy bars, whatever he has to). If we were to put Ace Hood's hustler up against Adderley's chain-gang worker we'd see some obvious differences. But what we'd see in both cases are black men who are forced to work incessantly with no way out. Both songs represent stylized attempts to deal with the nature of black labor in two different time periods.[2]

* * *

In the foreword I defined neoliberalism as the general idea that society works best when the people and the institutions within it work or are shaped to work according to market principles. We see this idea in public policy—in government attempts to privatize public resources (either by explicitly selling them off or by treating them as if they were privately rather than publicly owned). We see this idea in common sense accounts that routinely suggest businesses are better than governments at providing a range of services. We see this idea in seemingly non-political techniques designed to make individuals, populations, and institutions more entrepreneurial. What I haven't done is define what I mean by "the neoliberal turn". There was a time, decades ago, when the ideas, policies, and techniques associated with neoliberalism were viewed as radical. Now? Domestically and internationally we've got something close to a neoliberal consensus with political parties that are often on

---

2   It would be a full eleven years before Motown would release an album that contained songs as explicitly political as "Work Song" (Marvin Gaye's classic "What's Going On?", which Gordy only reluctantly released). Everything the label produced was arguably shaped by the politics and economics of labor. Of course the name "Motown" itself, the nickname blacks throughout the country gave Detroit, was derived from the auto industry ("MOtorTOWN"). But Gordy borrowed techniques from the assembly line in producing Motown's songs. Just like the automotive plants divided the process of car manufacturing into a number of discrete activities, Gordy cut up music production and distribution, separating out the processes of writing, singing, and playing music. The Funk Brothers were some of Motown's most productive and prolific session musicians. Oftentimes Gordy would have them come in and play music for songs that hadn't even been written yet, much less sung. And just like in the auto industry, after the final song was produced, a team of quality control specialists met to determine whether the final song was good enough to be released. Gordy even went so far as to tailor the sound quality of the song and the song length to the car radio audience (Smith 1999).

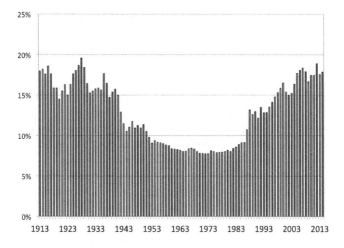

Figure 1. Top 1% Income Shares in the United States. Based on data from the World Top Incomes Database (Alvaredo et al. 2015) (http://www.wid. world), November 27, 2015.

the opposite ends of the spectrum agreeing on the necessity of neoliberal policies, ideas, and techniques of government. How did this happen? I begin with two graphs, one depicting levels of inequality from the early twentieth century to now (Figure 1), the other charting productivity alongside wages from 1973 to now (Figure 2, page 11).

From the beginning of the twentieth century to around 1929 the wealthiest Americans control a significant portion of America's wealth compared to the poorest. Then it drops, only to rise again around 1970...to the point that we have now the highest levels of inequality in the last one hundred years. Wealth is now extremely concentrated in the hands of a few—the net worth of the top 1% is 288 times the net worth of the average American family (Jacobs and Hacker 2008). What happened?

In the wake of the Great Depression, President Franklin D. Roosevelt, under pressure from activists, proposed and Congress passed what we now know as the New Deal. The New Deal gave labor the right to organize, it created unemployment insurance, it put people to work (on infrastructure projects, on data collection projects, on artistic projects) by creating the Workers Progress Administration,[3] and gave people baseline access to health insurance by creating Medicare. Finally, it supplemented the income of single mothers by creating Aid to Dependent Children (ADC).[4] The Second World War, as many deaths as it caused, put millions of men and women to work (including my maternal grandmother). After the war ended Congress passed the GI Bill, subsidizing the education and homeownership of millions of veterans. In the sixties Congress passed civil rights legislation making many forms of racial and gender discrimination illegal, and passed anti-poverty legislation designed to give resources to cities and health care to the poor.

These legislative acts were not possible without political struggle. Groups (political parties, laborers, unions, activists, businesses, women, African Americans) fought over proposing and passing these policies. Once these policies were passed, groups fought over how much funding they would receive and over how they would be implemented. And they fought over these things in part because they had different ideas about how to think about the problems the nation faced, and in part because they had different interests to protect (businesses wanted to protect their ability to make a profit, labor wanted to protect the ability of laborers to make a living off of their work, black men and women wanted to be treated as full citizens).

Partially through these acts, inequality fell significantly to the lowest levels of the modern era.

However, in the late sixties levels of inequality began to increase again.

While there are many different ways to define politics, with some focusing solely on elections and the like, and others focusing on a wide range of cultural activities, I define politics very simply as the group competition over scarce resources, as well as the various activities that comprise this competition. Every vote cast for one political candidate cannot, by definition, be cast for another political candidate. Every tax dollar

---

3   Later called the Work Projects Administration.
4   Which later became Aid to Families with Dependent Children (AFDC), which later became Temporary Aid to Needy Families (TANF).

spent on defense cannot be spent on welfare. Every minute spent debating legislation that would give more resources to single mothers cannot be spent on legislation that would give more resources to the dairy lobby. Every public policy dedicated to dealing with poverty cannot be dedicated to dealing with some other issue. These tangible resources—votes, money, time, public policy—are both incredibly important in structuring society[5] and are easy enough to wrap one's head around.

But we do not only fight over scarce tangible resources.

We also fight over resources that aren't quite as tangible.

For decades political scientists have studied "agenda-setting" as a central component of politics (Baumgartner and Jones 1993; Cohen 1999; Kingdon 1984). On the surface, an agenda is just a list of items a group needs accomplished and isn't "tangible" in the way that time, money, or votes are. However, agendas can only contain so many items, suggesting agenda items too are scarce resources. Further, to the extent agenda items represent problems that need to be solved, ideas people use to solve these problems can become resources groups fight over. Also, the way we fight—the rules of the competition itself—can become political terrain. How are votes counted? who is allowed to vote? how many votes does each individual receive?[6] I referred to public policy above, a term we take for granted. We also fight over the meaning and form of "the public"[7]—in fact, it may be one of the most important resources we fight over (and for).

---

5   One counter-response is that there are very few differences between political candidates, given the neoliberal turn. As I note later, the turn has broad bipartisan support. However, with that said, existing differences between political parties are still large enough on some issues—reproductive health looms large—that electing one slate of candidates vs. another could still result in very very different political outcomes.

6   In some democracies, for example, people are given a number of votes they can use to distribute between the candidates and parties of their choice. In the early nineties Lani Guinier (2002) was a strong proponent of this idea.

7   By "the public" I generally refer to three different connected concepts. First, "the public" is a community, a body of people that share membership in a political community (a city, a county, a state/province, a nation) or share a common identity. Second, "the public" is a set of resources that these people should share and have access to by dint of

Finally, in making decisions about time, money, votes, policies, agendas, the public, we use reason but we also use emotion—love, hate, disdain, derision. In deciding when, where, and how to act politically we routinely allot care to some groups while withholding it from others. There's more to politics, a lot more. But when I write about "politics", this is what I refer to. And when I talk about "black politics" I am referring to the ways different black populations compete over scarce resources, over time, over money, over votes, over public policy, over agenda items, over care, and other resources that have a significant impact on how black communities and the people within them are structured.

Politics is about competition over scarce resources. Politics is also, to an extent, about problem-solving. Inequality levels dropped around 1930 or so because of politics—because formerly less powerful groups fought against more powerful groups and won, changing legislation, changing public policy, changing political institutions, changing ideas about labor and the economy, about race, about citizenship, and, through these actions, changing the way material, social, and psychic resources were allocated. Now let's revisit those charts. How might we use politics to understand what happened?

Around 1972 two phenomena severely affected America and the rest of the developed world—high levels of unemployment and high levels of inflation.[8] This sent America and the rest of the industrialized world into an economic tailspin. The end result of this particular crisis was not just increased economic

---

their membership or identity. Here "the public" is synonymous with "the public good" or the idea that there is a community interest that benefits all of its individual members, and with "the commons" or the idea that there are shared community resources which cannot and should not be hoarded or made private. Third, "the public" is space designed for the community's general use (parks, gardens, public squares), sometimes for the specific purpose of generating discussion, debate, and decisions about issues of interest. In this latter instance the public can be a real space — a town hall for example — or it can be a virtual space (a public radio show).

8 Economists thought inflation was the function of high demand for goods and services, high demand that could only come if there were enough workers making a living to want the goods in the first place. It was supposedly impossible to simultaneously have this type of demand and high levels of unemployment. The events of the late sixties and early seventies proved them wrong.

anxiety and suffering. It was a crisis of ideas as well, in part because the theory routinely used to fix the economy proposed that we'd almost *never* have high levels of inflation and unemployment at the same time. High prices are usually the result of people spending a lot of disposable income on goods, and you don't have that when people are unemployed.

I noted that inequality began to drop as the result of political struggle. One of the things people struggled over was the discipline of economics. What economic theories best explained how economies worked and should work? Some political leaders and economists[9] suggested that it was the government's role to ensure that unemployment stayed relatively low by providing employment in times of severe economic crisis, and to provide citizens with resources (public education, unemployment, health care, retirement insurance) when citizens couldn't garner those resources through the market. And some political leaders and economists favored much more radical solutions.

Low levels of wealth inequality are very good for workers and for societies in general. People tend to have more options, they tend to be more mobile, they tend to live better lives. However, low levels of wealth inequality do not work particularly well for powerful business interests, nor do they work particularly well for the wealthy. If businesses have to pay workers high wages, if businesses have to spend valuable resources on making their workplace favorable to labor, their profit margin will significantly decrease. And the more legislative power labor has, the more likely the government collects and spends tax dollars on things that reduce business power and the power of the wealthy in general.

For a very specific group of intellectuals, this intellectual crisis—this inability to solve the economy using traditionally supported economic theory—became a political opportunity. They believed decreasing levels of inequality would give too

---

9   "Keynesians", named after British economist John Maynard Keynes. Keynesian economists argued that the actions of private actors alone could not keep an economy stable. Rather, government had to actively be engaged in the economy by setting policy and by spending money in times of recession.

much power to labor, would disrupt the generation of a supposed "free market", and as a result would kill capitalism.

So they took the opportunity presented by the crisis to roll out a different economic theory, one that proposed a very different relationship between the government and the market and between supply and demand. Whereas Keynesian economics suggested consumers were more important than producers and entrepreneurs (because entrepreneurs and businesses couldn't profit without consumers), and radical economists suggested that laborers were more important than business owners (small and otherwise), the new theory emphasized the importance of entrepreneurs and business owners (because if they didn't innovate, consumers wouldn't have jobs, and their society wouldn't progress). Whereas Keynesian economics suggested that governments should guide the economy in ways that would tend to lead to high levels of employment and productivity, and radical economics suggests that governments should guide the economy in ways that would tend to improve the course of human development, the new theory suggested these approaches would end up having the opposite effect.[10] The idea of human capital[11] theorized by the late Chicago economist Gary Becker plays a critical role here because it transforms labor from a simple unit you plug into an economic equation (so many units of labor translate into so much profit for the company when combined with so many units of equipment) into something human beings can themselves transform through skill development, education, creativity, and, perhaps most important of all, *choice*. Any attempt to use government to reduce the ability of business interests to make a profit, any attempt to use government to reduce the ability of entrepreneurs to innovate and create, any attempt to use government to artificially inflate or deflate the ability of an

---

10 If laborers, for example, *knew* that they couldn't be fired, they would be more irresponsible. Their irresponsibility in turn would reduce their productivity, which would in turn make societies worse off rather than better off. If governments attempted to plan every aspect of the economy they would eventually fail and devolve into totalitarianism.

11 The idea that human beings have a set of skills, values, and habits that they can develop to produce assets, just as classical economists believe businesses use capital to produce goods and services.

individual to profit off of his or her labor, were attempts to stifle freedom.[12]

Instead of reducing inequality by increasing government spending on infrastructure during downturns (hence stabilizing and perhaps increasing employment levels) or by providing public housing, unemployment insurance, a living wage, or other entitlements to citizens, people supporting these new ideas proposed that government dismantle such programs even if doing so increased inequality. Giving poor people and the unemployed resources actually makes them *more* poor and *more* reliant on the state rather than less (and hence *less free*), so we should cut the resources we give to them. Rather than provide poor single mothers with benefits to take care of their children, the new economic theory supported forcing single mothers to find work outside of the home. Because the new theory viewed the market as incredibly fragile, government should be used to bolster markets where they already existed and to create markets where they didn't exist. In fact, they argued government itself should be governed and critiqued by market standards — by how "efficient" it was, by how well it served its "customers", by how "entrepreneurial" various government actors behaved.

These ideas and the policies and techniques associated with them tend to increase levels of inequality. Further, they tend to "naturalize" inequality. That is, they tend to attribute inequality to personal, populational, or institutional flaws rather than structural ones. Even when politicians and policy makers do believe inequality is produced by structural factors, as a result of the neoliberal turn they are more likely to turn to the market for solutions than they are elsewhere. Indeed, and I write about this later, the very idea of "social entrepreneurship" revolves around the notion that we can somehow harness the wonders of the market to deal with social ills like poverty, hunger, and homelessness.

I want to go back to Ace Hood and the idea of the hustle above. The term's meaning changes 180 degrees because of the

---

12 For a fuller explanation of this story read Mark Blyth's work (2002, 2013).

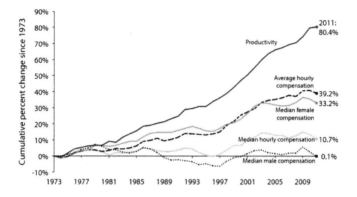

Figure 2. Productivity vs. Average Hourly Income (Economic Policy Institute 2012)

growing use of and acceptance of the concept of human capital. Indeed, under the neoliberal turn arguably the most important figure is the figure who consistently works. And the market becomes the most important venue with which the individual can figure out when to, where to, and how to develop his/her human capital, because only the market can give real time, dynamic, and accurate information about the context in which he/she can make human capital choices (when to go back to school, for example). In order to consistently provide for his mother, his child, as well as himself, Ace Hood has to be consistently working. Has to be consistently *productive*.

The above chart (Figure 2) traces increases over time in productivity, and then increases over time in wages. As we can see over the past several decades we've seen a steady rise in productivity. Compared to 1973, 2011 productivity had increased approximately 80%. But we are being paid far less in comparison. In fact, when we chart increases in productivity and wages together going back to the forties we find that they rise at about the same rate until around the same time inequality begins to spike again. After that point wages flat-line (Mishel 2012). The median average household income is $51,000. If this income rose at the same rate productivity did, it would now be approximately $91,000 (Gilson 2014). That is to say, if we took every American family and ranked them according to how much money they brought in, the family smack dab in the middle of that group would have almost twice as much money now if the money it brought in increased at the same rate its productivity did.

One way to explain the rise in productivity along with flattened wage rates is through globalization, through increased connections between countries like China and India and the United States. Compared to the 1950s, very few of our automobiles are produced by American workers. Rather, these and consumer goods like smartphones are increasingly produced outside of the United States and then imported back, in part because doing so enables American companies to produce these goods cheaper than if they were produced in the United States.

I mention smartphones. Another way to explain both the rise in inequality and the rising gap between productivity and wages is to explain it through increases in technology. Thinking about the automotive industry that made Motown possible, this sector is far more productive than it once was because the automation process made it possible to produce more cars more efficiently and less expensively. We can see this in any number of workplaces outside of the automotive plant. Increases in transportation technologies make it possible to create goods using overseas labor—it costs far less to ship goods in bulk to the US than it once did.

These increases in technology are also a partial function of globalization. Because of technological innovation in transportation it is possible to ship goods back and forth cheaper. Furthermore, because of the Internet it is now possible to outsource software development and engineering to nations like India for less than $10/hour through websites like virtualemployee.com (motto: "the future of work").

But technology didn't necessarily *have* to generate the gap between productivity and wages. We could have had a society in which wages and productivity increased at about the same rate. And globalization didn't necessarily have to generate this gap either. We could conceivably still have the type of global connectivity we now have while increasing wages domestically and globally.

The neoliberal turn explains this. Even as people are expected to be more and more productive, and like Ace Hood increasingly place more and more expectations upon themselves to be productive, the money they make as a result of that productivity flatlines, largely because of the way government (local, state, federal/national) ability to regulate businesses have been cut.

What are the effects of the two graphs? Again, we can get a sense of it by looking at the degree to which the hustler has become so important in hip-hop and in American popular culture in general. However, we can probably get a better sense of it by looking at labor. In the current moment four labor divides loom large: the divide between "good" and "bad" jobs; the divide between unionized and non-unionized jobs; the divide between the employed and unemployed; and the divide between the institutionalized and the non-institutionalized.

I begin with the "good job"/"bad job" divide. Good jobs offer benefits, good salaries, stable hours, job security, dignity, and safe working conditions. Unionized jobs in the auto or steel industry are good jobs. Many corporate managerial jobs are good jobs. Most programming jobs at places like Google are good jobs. My tenured job at a research university is a good job. People with these jobs can usually provide for themselves and their families, can get decent health care when they require it, have at least some due process in case of job disputes, and are given a degree of respect because of their job. These jobs require a great deal of human capital.

Bad jobs, on the other hand, offer very low wages, unstable hours, little to no job security, little to no dignity, no due process, unsafe working conditions, and little to no benefits. Jobs at Walmart and places like it tend to be bad jobs. Most temporary jobs are bad jobs, as they may offer decent wages but often offer no benefits and no job security. Unpaid internships, even ones that could lead to paid jobs, are also bad jobs (Lurie 2013). My first job at Wendy's, flipping burgers for $3.35/hour as a 15-year-old, was a bad job. Some adjunct faculty jobs are so bad they have to go on welfare, even though they have PhDs (Patton 2012). People working in these jobs are often just a hair above poverty, unable to fully provide for themselves or their families, unable to protect themselves or protest if they are fired, and unable to move to find better job opportunities.

The second divide is the divide between union workers and non-union workers.

Unions used to be a fixture of the American political and social landscape. The college educations my sister and I received were paid in part by my father's (union-supported) wages. Before manufacturing employment began to decrease, 35% of all American workers were part of a union. Near the end of President Ronald Reagan's first presidential term in 1984, approximately 20% of all wage and salary workers 16 years and older were unionized, compared to 2014 when only 11.1% of all wage and salary workers were unionized (Bureau of Labor Statistics). This drop largely comes from a drop in private sector union membership. In 1983 16.8% of private sector workers were members of a union, but in 2014 only 6.6% were.[13] In contrast, 35.7% of all public sector workers were members of unions in 2014, compared to approximately 37% in 1983.[14] As of 2014 most union workers are now public sector employees who work for federal, state, and local government rather than private sector employees who work for a private corporation like Ford or GM (Greenhouse 2011).

The good/bad and union/non-union distinctions are still about jobs. The third labor gap deals with unemployment. One of the most important and most analyzed aspects of the second great depression is the unemployment rate. But while high (as high as 10% in 2009), the conversation about unemployment does not begin to truly capture how dire this gap is, because the government doesn't define unemployment as the state of not having a job. Rather, the government defines unemployment as the state of not having a job *while actively looking for employment.*[15] This definition does not include people who have stopped looking for work.

---

13 Along these lines the union job my brother has came from my father as well.

14 I deal with education later, but one of the reasons why conservatives attack teachers' unions is because they constitute a large portion of public sector union workers.

15 Technically it is a bit more precise than that. People are defined as being "unemployed" if they are out of a job and have looked for work at least one of the preceding four weeks.

Further, the unemployment category doesn't begin to capture how the long-term unemployed are treated in the labor market. In a market where the number of people looking for jobs far outstrips the number of jobs available, employers have a significant degree of power to choose *exactly* who they want (often at lower wages than if the job market were better or if unions were stronger). Taking advantage of their power here, employers have begun discriminating against the long-term jobless (Krugman 2014). Indeed, this problem is so bad that a number of states have introduced legislation making it illegal for employers to discriminate against people based on their employment status.

The first two labor gaps distinguished between people with jobs. The third labor gap distinguishes between people with jobs and people without them. The fourth labor gap distinguishes between people counted in job data and people *who aren't counted in job data at all.*

Approximately 6.9 million Americans are either on parole, in prison, in jail, or on probation (Glaze and Kaeble 2014). The United States incarcerates more of its citizens than any other developed nation in the world, and many more than most underdeveloped nations as well. The United States has over twice as many prisoners serving life sentences (over 159,000), than Japan has *in prison* (60,486 as of 2014) (Institute for Criminal Policy Research, 2015; Nellis 2013).

We think about labor and work as being "productive", while we think of the unemployed as being "non-productive". To the extent we think about the incarcerated population, we think of them as being *counter-productive* rather than productive, that is, we view them as producing something (crime, disorder, violence) that hurts rather than benefits society. But there are at least two ways this account is complicated.

"Work Song" put to music an experience tens of thousands of black (and some white) prisoners dealt with throughout the first several decades of the twentieth century. Particularly in the Deep South, state officials would use prison labor to work on public and private projects cheaply, often timing arrests and imprisonments to coincide with corporate labor needs (Oshinsky 1996). This process has become modernized.

Corporations routinely use prison labor as a means of cheaply producing goods and services for consumers and for state government. California's Prison Industry Authority has an online catalog that sells a variety of prison-created products to state institutions, from a ceremonial indoor American flag with fringe (product number 495400.0000) for $60, to an assembled executive desk (product number 608500) for $90, to California prison uniforms (product number 406201.2080) for $32 (California Prison Industry Authority 2014). State law requires the prisoners be paid at least a minimum wage, but up to 80% of that wage goes to room and board and other bills.[16]

Secondly, in many states rural political districts count prisoners as residents of those districts for political representation purposes, even though these prisoners cannot vote in rural elections. Note how urban areas lose here. Several census blocks in urban areas are "million-dollar blocks", sending millions of dollars to the state and to rural districts in the form of prison labor, labor then counted in rural districts for the purposes of political representation.[17] Urban areas send thousands of bodies to rural districts for political representation. Upon freedom prisoners are often reluctant to engage in most forms of political participation and it is often incredibly difficult for former prisoners to find employment (Burch 2013; Weaver and Lerman 2010).

All of these labor divides are racialized.

As a direct result of housing segregation, blacks are concentrated in poor neighborhoods, cities, and educational systems. Unemployment is particularly concentrated in what we now think of as the Rust Belt, the former manufacturing hub of the country. Cleveland, Gary, Flint, Detroit, Baltimore, St. Louis, Milwaukee, all have incredibly high rates of unemployment and bad jobs (and high black populations). While cities like Seattle and New York City appear to thrive, in reality they are

---

16   If the prisoner is a father, for example, he is responsible for paying child support (Mink 1998).

17   The work of the Justice Mapping Center (www.justicemapping.org) is critically important here as they not only came up with the concept of the "million-dollar block"; they came up with an online tool that enables individuals to see for themselves how their neighborhood may be affected by the million-dollar block phenomenon.

good *and* bad job hubs.[18] Within metropolitan areas in general, unemployment is even more concentrated in poor non-white suburbs and neighborhoods.

During the nineties, white male and female job growth came almost solely from the growth in good jobs,[19] while approximately 75% of bad jobs went to African Americans and Latinos (Wright and Dwyer 2000). In fact, 3 out of every 5 jobs that were added among black and Latino populations were bad jobs. Currently there is a slight racial gap in union membership. Unionization rates for blacks and Asian Americans are high compared to their overall population percentage. Unionization rates for whites and Latinos, on the other hand, are low—and for whites, extremely low. And there has always been a large gap in employment rates, with the black unemployment consistently twice as high as white unemployment. Finally, over half of the (growing) incarcerated population is African American. Sending blacks to jail by the tens of thousands, taking away their voting rights, and then counting them as citizens for the purpose of white, rural, and conservative political representation, represents a form of economic and political exploitation. Many if not most of our nation's "million-dollar blocks" are black blocks.[20]

The contemporary nature of these divides is largely the product of the neoliberal turn.

The divide between good jobs and bad jobs comes from deindustrialization, which itself comes from public policy designed to first entice manufacturers to move out of industrial centers

---

18 New York City's financial managers, lawyers, doctors, entertainers, and entertainment executives need bike messengers, taxi cab drivers, dry cleaners, waiters, concierge service, janitors, landscapers, jobs that pay very very little and offer even fewer benefits.

19 White women were especially able to take advantage of the market. Not only did they outpace their white male counterparts in their ability to find jobs, they outpaced their white male counterparts in their ability to find *good* jobs.

20 It is possible to overstate this dynamic. One of the myths black people routinely spread about the plight of black men is that there are more black men in prison than there are in college. Now, even given the fact that undergraduate college students tend to be between 18–22 while incarcerated men range in age from 18 (and less in some cases) to 80, there are still fewer black men in prison than there are in college.

(with high labor costs) and then secondly to reduce international trade barriers in ways that reduce labor costs even more.[21] But this divide is also increasingly supported by our own growing acceptance of the idea of human capital. If human capital is something we work on and make choices to develop, just like businesses, then the benefits we receive or do *not* receive are the result of our choices. In other words, people who work at Walmart "deserve" to work at Walmart, and "deserve" the low wages they are given. People who work at Google, on the other hand, not to mention the people who created Google in the first place, "deserve" the high wages (and stock dividends) they receive. Why, using this logic, would we pay someone the equivalent of a middle-class salary and benefits to engage in nothing more than routine physical labor?

The divide between union and non-union jobs can be viewed through a similar lens. I distinguished good jobs from bad jobs by wages, job security, benefits, dignity, and due process. These came from union activism. Through collective bargaining, unions made it possible for most blue and white-collar employees to make good wages, be treated with dignity, have concrete ways to deal with conflict and workplace harassment, and to work under safe conditions. Even now, people in unions get paid on average much better wages than people not in unions, across all sectors (US Bureau of Labor Statistics 2010). In part because unions are so weak, undereducated workers (and, increasingly, workers in general) find it hard to provide a decent living for their families. Reducing the strength of unions did not eradicate good jobs entirely. Google, for

---

21   The beginning of the trend actually occurred in the fifties as the federal government subsidized relocating manufacturers away from the Midwest and the North-central regions of the country in response to what they perceived to be the growing Communist threat, but it really began to take hold in the seventies as a direct result of the late sixties/early seventies economic crisis. Before this moment, even given the shrinking jobs in the manufacture sector, it was still possible for men with less than a high school degree to find employment with good salaries, benefits, and dignity. White men were able to get more of these jobs than other racial groups, but because of civil rights era gains blacks were able to find jobs this way as well, particularly in places like Detroit. By the mid to late seventies this pretty much dried up — unemployment levels and relatively uneducated men in these regions increased and their salaries decreased (Bound and Holzer 1993).

example, tends to pay workers well, tends to offer good benefits, and creates the type of workspace many of us would dream of, although Google's employees are not unionized. However, as unions decreased the number of mid-range jobs decreased also. Further, the number of "bad jobs" increased, with "bad" becoming "worse".

Human capital is an individual trait, not necessarily a collective one. Neoliberal logic suggests unions distort the ability of markets to function perfectly by taking away the ability of individuals to negotiate their wages based on their own human capital. Further, unions distort their ability to function on the job because the benefits unions provide can make people less likely to work hard (or at all). This logic is reflected in decisions at both the national and state level that reduce the ability of unions to form or negotiate. Here I'd also include the legislation that reduces international trade barriers.

The divide between the employed and the unemployed is also connected to the concept of human capital, as human capital can both be used to explain why some people are employed and some people are *not*, and to argue for certain types of solutions as opposed to others. If the reason people are unemployed is not because of structural deficits or discrimination but because they haven't done what it takes to be employed, then the solution is for them to somehow *attain* the needed skills to become competitive on the job market. Here the ascension of neoliberal economics is particularly acute. The reason unemployment is high during recessions is because companies do not have the profit base required to sustain a full suite of employees. The only entity with the ability to hire and put money into the economy when private businesses don't (or more accurately, *won't*) is the government.

These labor divides reduce the ability of individuals within the various segments to fight for singular political alternatives because they each have different interests. They also tend to concentrate what political successes occur within the higher end of the labor spectrum because those at the top of the various divides tend to have relatively more political resources than those at the bottom.

The neoliberal turn began in 1972 during Richard Nixon's presidency. However, the American political figure most associated with the turn is Ronald Reagan. Given how long ago

Reagan was in office, it is worth dealing with how transformative a figure he was. Before Reagan's election, government
spending on public housing had increased significantly. After
his election, he stopped construction of new public housing units. He cut full-time Housing and Urban Development
(HUD) staff by 21% and restructured it by making it a voucher
program,[22] and by the middle of his second term had reduced
public housing by 80% compared to 1982. Reagan reduced
unemployment benefits by $4.6 billion in 1983 *alone.* Reagan
weakened labor by killing the air traffic controllers strike of
1981 (Shostak 2006), and then by appointing men and women
with strong anti-labor positions to the National Labor Relations
Board (NLRB), who then reversed several previous pro-labor
decisions. Reagan significantly reduced the ability of the government to raise taxes by making deficits a political issue, by
generating broad support for tax cuts (even though the prime
beneficiaries of those tax cuts were wealthier Americans), and
by reducing the ability of state and local governments to collect taxes — this even as he both cut aid to local governments
and cut resources to organizations created for the purpose of
promoting local government interests (Conlan 1998; Pierson
1994; Waidref 2008). Finally, in addition to the policy changes
he instituted and the legislation he supported, he consistently
promoted the idea that government was *the* problem rather
than the solution to the ills society faced.

Ronald Reagan transformed the way we think about government, and this not only affected the Republican Party, it
affected the Democratic Party. Every Democratic president
we've elected since Reagan has promoted neoliberal ideas
and policies. It wasn't a Republican who ended welfare: it was
Bill Clinton.[23] As I show in chapter 4, George W. Bush helped

---

22 Vouchers are a key aspect of neoliberal policy transformation as they
    marketize public goods.
23 We now look backwards to the Clinton era with fondness because we
    think it was a particularly good time for the economy. Unemployment
    rates were as low as 4%, incredibly low by current standards.
        However, this backwards glance is rose-colored.
        Most of the jobs created during this period were either very good
    or very bad. Approximately 40% of the job growth during the nineties
    came from either very good (20%) or very bad jobs (17%) (Wright and

neoliberalize public education (with No Child Left Behind), and Barack Obama continued rather than stopped this attempt (with Race to the Top). And an array of policy experts, local political officials, and even in some cases political activists have promoted neoliberal ideas and policies. Over the past few years a number of people with progressive politics have begun to tout GoFundMe and Kickstarter as ways to sidestep the significant lack of resources activists often have to pursue progressive political ends. These applications and others like them require individuals to treat their cause as if it were an economic product, and their personal network as a potential "market".

It makes sense that a group of people and institutions interested in hoarding and accumulating wealth would promote policies that also promoted their self-interest. But what doesn't make sense is the support these policies receive from regular everyday citizens. *Why* were the various policies and ideas proposed predominantly by business interests and by conservatives taken as gospel from people who were hurt by them? Some knew that the effects of these policies would be disastrous on the working class. And surely once people like Reagan began to actually *implement* these strategies it should have been *clear* that these policies would have horrific consequences. Yet the American populace still supported them. What happened to get the American populace to support them in such large numbers?

Racial politics.

As inequality increases, the number of societal "losers"— individuals who can't make ends meet, who simply cannot

---

Dwyer 2000). By comparison, less than 2% of the growth in overall jobs came from the growth in very bad jobs in the sixties. This pattern has gotten even worse since the Clinton era. Traditionally, temporary agencies are responsible for a very low percentage of jobs. But as of summer 2013, temporary agencies were responsible for the most jobs (Wright 2013). The end result of this divide is that we're swiftly becoming a nation where, if you have a job, you either have a Walmart job welcoming customers as they walk in (and are likely participating in a multi-level marketing program like Mary Kay or Avon to make extra money), or you work at Google, with little to no room in between.

succeed on society's terms, try as they might—also increases. The public policy developed to deal with these populations becomes increasingly punitive, increasingly cordoning off these populations from the rest of society, increasingly reducing the resources they have access to, increasingly forcing them to undergo government surveillance and control in exchange for those few resources they receive, and increasingly leaving them to die when they are unable to behave "responsibly". Increasingly exposing populations to pain and suffering the way neoliberalism does can only occur under very specific circumstances. Somehow, members of society must be convinced that losers deserve what they get, that they lose not because the deck is stacked against them but rather because they have something wrong with them that can only be dealt with punitively. And they must see themselves in the winners. Similarly, they must begin to think that the "public good", particularly in the form of increased taxes and service provision, is the equivalent of theft.

Racial politics perform work here, as white attitudes about labor, work, crime, and taxes are fused to attitudes about black men and women and, through them, to other non-white populations. As a result, a wide variety of public institutions and public goods come under attack. It isn't that people begin to hate "big government", as this is technically inaccurate. It's that people begin to simultaneously hate government programs that offer progressive assistance to populations perceived to be undeserving *and* desire government programs that punish these populations. Under neoliberalism people increasingly support spending resources on imprisoning (black) criminals, on border protection against (Latino/a) immigrants, and on protecting our infrastructure from (Middle Eastern) terrorists.

The racial differences within each of these important labor divides hurt American populations in general. They increase housing segregation that in turn exacerbates inequality. They increase negative attitudes about poor and working class populations—if people in "good jobs" tend to live in distinctly different neighborhoods than other populations, they are not likely to be exposed to them, causing them to develop attitudes about this population through the media or through random (negative) personal encounters. Race does a tremendous amount of work in generating public support for punitive policies. Even for the unemployed.

Take the following comment made in 2012 by Representative Blake Farenthold (R-TX) at a community meeting:

> Drug testing for recipients of various welfare programs, I really think that's something that needs to be considered. We've gotta, you know, nobody wants to starve anybody. Everybody wants to help folks out. But we've got a system where you can stay on unemployment for an awfully long time. And I think we need to create a system of decreasing benefits over time to encourage you to get a job. I think anybody who's had an alcoholic in their life or somebody with a drug problem, realizes that until things get bad enough there's no incentive to change. I think that we're so generous in some of our social problems that people are unwilling to get a job outside in the heat. Rather than get 15 dollars to go get [a roofing job] ... they'd rather get 9 or 10 dollars in benefits. I think drug testing is not an unreasonable requirement to get benefits. (Jilani 2014)

First note his comment about unemployment. "You can stay on unemployment for an awfully long time." Compared to what? During the current recession Congress passed legislation to allow unemployed men and women to collect benefits for up to 73 weeks (depending on the state), but the normal maximum (which states have now gone back to) is 26 weeks. This is half the maximum Germany allows for younger unemployed workers, and only one quarter what France allows for unemployed workers. Second, note how he connects unemployment to drug addiction. For him the unemployed need to hit rock bottom by being forced to work.

Arguing that unemployment benefits (which only pay a fraction of the worker's original salary) last too long and that the unemployed need to be treated like drug addicts and forced to work is easier to do when the people listening already believe that the unemployed are stereotypically lazy and shiftless.[24] I referred to the ways various Democratic presidents reproduced neoliberal ideas. Although the rise in the number of the incarcerated begins in the early seventies, we really see an increase after Bill Clinton signs the Violent Crime Control and Law Enforcement Act (Feldman et al. 2001). None of these labor gaps would be as significant as they are if the federal government paid for college education, for example, thereby easing parental anxiety about paying for their children's education, or paid a minimum income or provided universal health care. But not only do we *not* have a robust welfare state, Clinton cut back what we had when he repealed welfare by signing the Personal Responsibility Work Opportunity Reconciliation Act, which transformed a lifetime right to a temporary privilege (with significant strings attached).[25] And he was able to make the cutbacks because people associate welfare with black women (Gilens 1999). Indeed, Clinton signed the bill with two single black mothers on federal assistance standing by his side. Compared to whites, blacks have less income, less wealth, less education. They tend to live in poorer neighborhoods and tend to be sicker than their white counterparts. And, compared to whites, blacks tend to benefit far less from a variety of "submerged state" tax expenditures than their white counterparts.[26]

24 An economist recently ran an experiment creating resumes for 4800 fictitious job candidates. The resumes only differed by the amount of time the fictitious candidates had been unemployed. The results were telling. The fictitious candidates unemployed for more than six months received very few callbacks compared to the fictitious candidates who'd been unemployed for less time (O'Brien 2013). Even though more long-term unemployed are white rather than non-white (Mitchell 2013), the language of race extends to the long-term unemployed to the point where some could argue that the unemployed are now "black".

25 In some states, for example, women had to take paternity tests in order to qualify for the temporary aid. In most states women had to actively look for work. Joe Soss, Richard Fording, and Sanford Schram (2011) definitively show that these and other punitive measures were connected to race — states and counties with larger black populations were far more likely to have punitive welfare policies than other states.

26 Suzanne Mettler's (2011b) work is important here. The home-mortgage interest deduction alone is worth over $100 billion dollars. But while a program like Food Stamps (which in 2010 dollars costs less than half the home-mortgage interest deduction) is condemned *at best*, the home-mortgage deduction continues without critique.

While 99% of all citizens need progressive government and need government programs that actively provide income and other resources to poor and working class populations, black citizens arguably need them more and are wounded more when they don't exist.

This brings us to black politics.

If we were to compare levels of "white inequality" over time with levels of "black inequality" (that is, inequality within black communities), what we find is there is actually more inequality *within* black communities than there are within white ones. Well-off black families tend to have a larger share of the resources than not-so-well-off black families have . . . and *this* share is larger than the share well-off white families have in relationship to not-so-well-off white families. I by no means want to suggest that intra-racial and inter-racial inequality are the same; they are not. Whites have much more wealth than blacks (Conley 1999; Oliver and Shapiro 1995). However, focusing solely on inter-racial inequality causes us to erase the inequality that exists *within* black communities.

And this causes us to gloss over the fact that neoliberal ideas and policies are not simply produced and reproduced by whites to withhold resources from blacks. Black institutions and ideas have themselves been transformed. Black elected officials and civil rights leaders reproduce these ideas, participating in a remobilization project of sorts, one that consistently posits that the reason black people aren't as successful as their white counterparts is because of a lack of hustle, is because they don't quite have the work ethic necessary to succeed in the modern moment. A remobilization project that consistently posits that the greatest danger black people face is one posed by other black people, black people who are not only *not* productive but are in fact *counter-productive.* This remobilization project posits that there are two types of black people — black people who have the potential to be successful if they take advantage of their human capital, and black people who have no such potential.

This is one of the biggest hurdles we have to face in the early decades of the twenty-first century.

2

The city is the base which we must organize as the factories were organized in the 1930's. We must struggle to control, to govern the cities, as workers struggled to control and govern the factories of the 1930's.
—Grace and James Boggs (1970, p. 46)

The *right to the city* cannot be conceived of as a simple visiting right or as a return to traditional cities. It can only be formulated as a transformed and renewed *right to urban life*.
—Henri Lefebvre (1996, p. 158)

I BEGAN THE LAST CHAPTER WITH THE HUSTLE. THOUGH WE CAN technically find evidence of "the hustle" everywhere, it's difficult to imagine a record like Ace Hood's "Hustle Hard" taking place anywhere other than in an urban neighborhood. While it is indeed possible to "hustle" in rural areas, the city provides unique opportunities simply not available anywhere else. In this chapter I want to tackle the city explicitly.

I begin with two quotes from urban organizer-theorists. Grace and James Boggs were some of the first people to recognize that the growing obsolescence of industrial labor had a very particular effect on black urban workers and on what we now know as the Rust Belt. Their essay "The City is the Black Man's Land" was written in 1966 about Detroit and cities like it. Henri Lefebvre is best known for his work on the production of space. In his essay "The Right to the City" (written just a few months before student protests in France) he argued that people who lived in the city had more right to construct and reconstruct it than people/corporations who technically owned it.

27

Both the Boggs and Lefebvre understood that the city was ground zero for the development of alternative ways of life. And they understood that cities like Paris and Detroit did not just grow naturally—rather, they were the product of larger economic, political, and social forces that threatened to reduce them to capital hubs.

These forces are crucial to the development of what George Clinton (1975) calls "chocolate cities". Two forces loomed large in the early half of the twentieth century. The first was growing industrialization. Black laborers migrated to cities like Detroit to meet the labor needs of manufacturers like Ford. The second was war.

During World War II American political elites recognized that veterans had to be given more resources in order to compensate them for their sacrifice and to maintain support for the military. In recognition of this they passed the GI Bill, which provided US veterans with free education and inexpensive housing (provided the housing was built outside of the city). And, with the threat of Soviet Union missile strikes looming large, they realized they needed to decentralize America's industrial capacity. This meant moving industry out of major cities like Detroit and into the suburbs. In recognition of this they passed the National Interstate and Defense Highways Act[1] of 1956, which significantly reduced the resources corporations needed to create new (suburban and rural) plants and to ship goods from one part of the country to the other.[2]

Before these bills, cities like Detroit concentrated labor, capital, and productive capacity. The GI Bill and Interstate Highways Act reversed this dynamic. GIs prevented from building new homes in the cities moved into suburbs. The nation's plants were relocated and rebuilt in the suburbs. It's important to note the racial consequences of these two policies. Although

---

1   Yes, the *Defense Highways Act*. Our freeways are the product of and designed for war.

2   The Big Three did not just simply take old plants and move them into the rural hinterlands. They updated the plants. Because land was cheaper in rural areas than urban ones they were able to build outward rather than up. Further, they were able to automate their plants, which significantly reduced their need for (unionized) labor.

the GI Bill was not explicitly discriminatory—black GIs had as much right to the resources given by the bill that their non-black counterparts did—suburbs throughout the nation racially discriminated against blacks (Katznelson 2005). Further, although race was not at the forefront of the decision to decentralize America's "arsenal of democracy", moving plants to white-only suburbs further segregated the nation and concentrated unemployment within urban (now predominantly black) communities all throughout the Rust Belt. Many of the suburbs created to house the new plants and new middle-class populations were racially exclusive, precluding blacks and other racial minorities from moving into them.

These two forces hastened the development of chocolate cities and, in the sixties, conspired to create a powerful stew. White and capital flight, made possible by the GI Bill and the Interstate Highway Act, combined with the increasing influx of black and brown populations, crystallized growing urban poverty and unemployment. In the sixties, cities exploded in dozens of race riots—over 125 rebellions in response to Martin Luther King Jr.'s assassination alone (McAdam 1982). In reaction to this and to growing political activism, Lyndon Johnson's Great Society program spent billions on anti-poverty programs often, bypassing state and local governments in doing so. But by the early seventies, with the onset of the neoliberal turn, support for these programs began to wither.

Richard Nixon's presidency becomes important here for several reasons, but I want to focus on four.

Internationally, it was under Nixon's watch that we see the first (forceful) application of neoliberal policy. The first nation to actually try to put neoliberal policies in practice was Chile.[3] But the Chilean government didn't implement these policies democratically. The Chilean government was overthrown by its military, who then—through University of Chicago–trained

---

3   These included privatizing social security, slashing government regulations, and removing trade restrictions, all of which had the effect of increasing wealth inequality and significantly decreasing the quality of life of Chile's poorest citizens.

Chilean economists—implemented the reforms. Nixon supported the coup.

Domestically, Nixon was the first president to begin to use the same methods of analyzing government effectiveness that businesses used.[4] While this seems to make a great deal of common sense, inasmuch as there are a variety of aspects of government that can't effectively be measured (the importance of clean air and water for example), the more this approach is adopted, the harder it becomes to make a claim for a uniquely "public" domain that shouldn't be treated the same way as one would treat the private market.

He was also the first president to adopt "the southern strategy", a campaign strategy designed to build support for the Republican party through racist appeals to white voters. There's a long history going all the way back to the Reconstruction of white elites convincing working class white voters that they should *not* support progressive government. The "southern strategy" represented the late twentieth-century version of this model, as Nixon convinced white working class voters that progressive government was by definition corrupt in part because it increased black lawlessness.

Finally, although he didn't do this on purpose, his involvement in and subsequent resignation due to the Watergate scandals significantly dampened support for government.

The end result of Nixon's approach? When the economic crisis of the seventies hit, unemployment in cities, already high because of plant relocation and automation,[5] exploded.

---

4   In policy terms, this led Nixon to support three different moves. First, he supported a set of reforms designed to simplify the often complicated relationship between federal, state, and local governments. Second, he supported combining a number of smaller grants into larger "block" grants that could be given to state and local governments to use as they wished (within limits). Third, he supported revenue sharing—returning to state and local governments a percentage of the revenue that they paid out in taxes. The three policy changes in tandem kept the relationship between the federal government and other levels of government and the purpose of that relationship more or less intact.

5   Industrial corporations did not simply take their urban plants and relocate them to the suburbs; they used the opportunity to modernize, and they did this largely by introducing automated labor that had the effect of significantly reducing their labor needs.

As the nation became more and more suburban and urban areas began to be perceived (and depicted) as drains on the economy (in large part because of their increasingly black population), the country was incredibly receptive to the idea that blacks and corrupt liberals were responsible. The growing concentration of poor and unemployed blacks was increasingly viewed as the crisis of progressive government *itself* rather than being viewed as a crisis of the lack of progressive government.

As a result of white and capital flight, city revenues began to decrease, even as demands for social services *increased.* Cities turned to the market, relying more and more on municipal bonds to generate revenue. These bonds were rated by bond agencies. Bonds with low ratings are worth little more than junk. Bonds with high ratings are viewed as being top-notch investments. In 1960 tax-exempt municipal bonds only accounted for 21.6% of bank portfolios in 1960. Within less than fifteen years, this number had increased to 50% as cities began to rely on them a lot more (Tabb 1982). Their increased reliance on bonds made cities hostage to the bond rating agencies. If bond rating agencies gave less favorable ratings to cities interested in neighborhood development, cities didn't float bonds for that purpose.

The case of New York City is illustrative.

In the mid-seventies, New York City experienced a significant budget crisis. New York City Mayor Abraham Beame appealed to the state and federal governments, following the trend established by his predecessor and other big city mayors. Republican state legislators refused to give the city the levels of state aid it needed, and President Ford refused to give federal aid.

The result was one of the first modern austerity experiments. The state of New York created an Emergency Financial Control Board (EFCB), composed of the governor, the mayor, the state's and city's comptrollers, and three corporate leaders selected by the governor. The purpose of the EFCB? To control all of the city's budgetary decisions, taking these decisions away from local elected officials. While it was designed to be temporary, an "emergency" failsafe of sorts, after 1978 "emergency" was removed from its title.

It's worth considering the costs of this decision.

> Between January 1, 1975, and May 31, 1976, the city payroll was cut by 25 percent, the sanitation department by close to that, and schools by slightly more. A 13.7 percent cut in the number of police meant, according to the mayor, 'substantial decreases in enforcement efforts'.... Fire department response time increased by a factor of four. Hospitals were closed, and in many sections only one nurse was on duty.... In 1975, 15,000 teachers and paraprofessionals — constituting 20 percent of union membership — were laid off, and this reduced the proportion of black and Spanish-surnamed teachers from 11 to 3 percent — remember that two-thirds of the *students* are black or Spanish-surnamed.... Between the fall of 1974 and the winter of 1976, the city workforce lost half its Spanish-surnamed workers, two-fifths of its black male employees, and one-third of its female employees. (Tabb 1982, p. 30)

By the end of this period, New York City, one of the most progressive cities in the country, had become one of the least progressive. I'll just focus on one issue — that of higher education. The City University of New York (CUNY) system provided free college educations to tens of thousands of poorer black, brown, and white citizens. In order to make the system more "efficient", political elites added tuition without significantly increasing financial aid. As a result, between 1974 and 1980, the system had 80,000 fewer students. The "right to the city" had been effectively transferred. New York City had been transformed from a city designed at least in part to meet the needs of its residents, to a city designed to meet the needs of its investors.

New York City Mayor Beame's replacement, Ed Koch, not only accepted the work of the Financial Control Board, he touted it, explicitly redefining the purpose of the city to fit the new context. According to Mayor Koch, the role of the city was *not* to provide services for its residents; the role of the city was to create the proper climate for business development.

The policy solution New York adopted swiftly became the new normal.

When Ronald Reagan was elected president he took this approach national, reducing federal spending on domestic priorities in general, placing a far greater burden on state and local governments to tackle domestic issues while also making it much harder for states and local governments to do so.[6]

When people elected Bill Clinton in 1992, some thought that Clinton would reverse this. And he did in a few ways — he raised taxes, for instance,[7] and significantly increased the number of African American political appointees. However, Clinton also aggressively promoted the idea that government worked best when it worked according to market principles. In 1993 he created the National Partnership for Reinventing Government, a public-private task force comprised of corporate leaders and political officials for this purpose. Touting the initiative, he consistently referred to citizens as consumers, emphasized corporate innovation and entrepreneurialism over government inefficiency, and touted waste reduction and efficiency over almost every other organizational principle. The effect of the rhetoric above and beyond the actual policy prescriptions was to radically alter the way citizens thought about government and to radically alter the way citizens thought of citizenship *itself*. But in addition to the rhetoric the task force led to a significant reduction in government employees, combined with a significant increase in the responsibility government employees had to bear.

---

6   Between 1980 and 1985, Reagan reduced all outlays to state and local government by almost 24%, outlays in the area of community and regional development by approximately 40%, for educational training and service by approximately 33%, and general purpose assistance by 45% (Conlan 1998, p. 147). Reagan also reduced their ability to collect taxes and their lobbying capacity. This forced them to fight against the mandates and to increasingly turn to business interests to help shore up the shortfall in revenues.

7   Technically Reagan did this too, but Reagan was forced to do so and, even as he raised taxes, rarely veered from rhetoric suggesting that taxes were the problem rather than the solution.

In 1994, he sought to apply this approach to cities by creating urban "empowerment zones".[8] Empowerment zones would receive federal grants and special tax abatements designed to increase local business investment and employment. Unlike Reagan's approach, empowerment zones were partially funded by the federal government. However, like Reagan's approach, federal funding was limited — not every city and rural area that could have potentially benefitted from the empowerment zone designation received one. So a competition was established. Local governments would compete for empowerment zone status by drafting a proposal outlining what they would do if they were awarded EZ status. The proposal had to reflect not only government participation but bank, business, non-profit,

---

8   Of all days, Clinton announced the initiative on the Martin Luther
     King Jr. holiday in 1994:

> This empowerment zone initiative, therefore, is a central part of a
> broadly coordinated strategy. With business people in mind, the
> plan seeks to make places more attractive for new investment so
> that people can — Arland Smith can fulfill their dreams. We built
> about $2.5 billion in tax incentives into this plan. They say if you
> hire a new worker in this zone, you'll get a tax break. If you retrain
> a worker who lives in this zone, you'll get a tax break. In other
> words, the plan rewards people for results, for reaching people in
> communities that presently are seeing disinvestment instead of
> new investment.
>
> It's much better than welfare, and it recognizes that it doesn't
> make any economic sense for us to be trying to build new markets
> all around the world when we have huge, untapped, undeveloped
> markets right here at home: millions and millions and millions
> of potential consumers for American products and services who
> cannot be part of the American market because they, themselves,
> do not have the education, the training, the jobs, and the supports
> that they need. If we simply can apply our international economic
> policy to south central Los Angeles, Harlem, Milwaukee, Detroit,
> you name it, the Mississippi Delta, south Texas, we're going to
> do just fine in this country. We should see the American people
> who have the ability of this fine young man who just spoke as an
> enormous asset that we are not tapping. And we have no excuses
> now for not doing it, because we know better, and we know it. How
> many times did I give that speech during the NAFTA debate? The
> only way a rich country grows richer is to find more people who
> buy its products and services. In America we have millions of peo-
> ple who don't buy our products and services, because we have not
> invested in them and their potential and created the conditions in
> which they can succeed. So that is what this is all about. (Clinton
> 1994)

and community participation as well. Cities able to compete were rewarded, in this case with tax credits, with block grant money for social service provision, and with waivers from federal regulations. Both the rewards and the application process itself were designed to make cities more amenable to businesses and to "public-private partnerships" that would further force cities to act according to market principles.

We see Clinton apply a similar but much more punitive approach to poor populations. Two pieces of legislation stand out.

In 1994, the same year he proposed the creation of empowerment zones, Clinton signed the Violent Crime Control Act. Although Ronald Reagan is responsible for the biggest percentage increase in prison funding and incarceration rates, Bill Clinton is responsible for the largest absolute increase in prison funding and incarceration rates (Alexander 2010; Burch 2013; Clear and Frost 2013; Wacquant 2009). The act increased the number of federal crimes, and gave almost $10 billion in state funds to support new prison development. Before the passage of the bill, prisoners could receive a Pell Grant to either begin or continue education while in prison, and people with criminal records were still eligible for public resources (like public housing, for example). The bill discontinued the practice, which eradicated the ability of poorer prisoners to educate themselves while in prison, and made people with records ineligible for public resources.

Two years later Clinton signed the Personal Responsibility Work Opportunity Reconciliation Act (PRWORA). While Reagan rhetorically condemned people on welfare—in fact, Reagan helped popularize the concept of the "welfare queen"—he never successfully killed welfare policy. The act effectively did what Reagan couldn't, replacing a permanent program designed to give resources to poor single mothers and their children (Aid to Families of Dependent Children or AFDC—itself a replacement for Aid to Dependent Children) with a temporary program (Temporary Aid to Needy Families or TANF). Rather than being held hostage by the Republican Party, Clinton *ran for office promising to "end welfare as we know it"*.

With TANF, the primary goal of welfare becomes transitioning women to work, as opposed to providing the benefits they need to take care of themselves and their children. States remain important in determining benefits and requirements. But under TANF, local jurisdictions *within* states could shape and determine their own rules and levels of benefits—between 1996 and 2001 fourteen states decided to give local authorities significant control over benefits (Soss et al. 2011). However, this came with strings—by law states and local jurisdictions cannot offer *more* benefits without facing significant federal penalties.[9] Further, while states and local jurisdictions were given incentives to experiment, they are given more incentives to experimentally punish than experimentally reward.[10] Finally, under TANF fathers become financially responsible for their children, and the father must pay back any benefits the state provides to his children in his absence.[11] Clinton institutionalized a

---

9   If Baltimore, for example, wanted to give teenage single mothers more benefits, given the particular burden they have to face in taking care of their children, they can only do so if they either withhold benefits from another potential beneficiary group or if they suffer penalties from either the State of Maryland, the federal government, or both.

10   Because black people have always been more likely to be poor, race has significantly shaped the form and function of welfare. Arguably, one of the reasons we even think of welfare as synonymous with AFDC is because we now routinely associate black people with "being on the dole", so to speak, as opposed to benefiting from Social Security or Unemployment Insurance, much less from aspects of the hidden or submerged welfare state like the home mortgage interest deduction or 401k programs (Howard 1997; Mettler 2011). But research suggests a negative relationship between black population size and ADC payments—as black population size increased ADC payments *decreased* (Lieberman 1998). Because blacks were more likely to require ADC than whites, this relationship is the exact opposite of what we would expect given black poverty. Further, as the image shifts—and as newspapers increasingly depict welfare recipients as black rather than as white—white support for welfare drops and white support for punitive responses to poverty increases (Gilens 1999). When TANF becomes the law of the land, research definitively shows a relationship between state black population size and the willingness of the state to give control to local jurisdictions *and* a relationship between black population size and the willingness of states to adopt increasingly punitive measures to get welfare recipients to work (Soss et al. 2011).

11   Indeed, if a mother either doesn't want to have a relationship with the father of her children, does not know the father of her children, or does not wish to place financial responsibility onto the father, her benefits will be withheld (Mink 1998).

program that ignores the work mothers perform in the home, and forces poor women (and indirectly poor men) to take full economic responsibility for their reproductive health choices. Whereas we routinely laud the idea of stay-at-home mothers, recognizing that children tend to do better if at least one parent can spend quality time looking to their needs, we castigate poor women for making that decision.

The bill wreaked havoc on poor communities and did little to nothing to reduce the stigma of "welfare", did nothing to kill the stereotype of the welfare queen, and did nothing to reduce poverty levels (Mink 1998; Schram 2000, 2006). It ended a longstanding right to aid from the government, replacing it with a temporary "privilege" that could only be received if the recipient behaved correctly. It made women on it take more and more responsibility for finding employment (as if being a single mother wasn't job enough) by withholding resources from them until they proved they were doing so, and then on top of that by placing a five-year *lifetime* limit on their benefits.

When Bill Clinton signs the PRWORA he does so flanked by two single black mothers. This isn't a coincidence. Echoing the "southern strategy" used to build the modern day Republican Party, Clinton relied heavily on racist images of black women and black men to consistently increase support for punitive approaches to crime and welfare, images that exerted a powerful effect on public opinion (Gilens 1999; Gilliam Jr. et al. 2002; Hurwitz and Peffley 1997; Kinder and Sanders 1996; Peffley et al. 1997).

Clinton did what Reagan couldn't do on welfare. He did what Reagan began to do on crime. Further, while Clinton did not go quite as far as Reagan did in castigating the role of government, he did go farther than Reagan did in arguing that government should do more to model itself like a business and that the relationship between government and citizen should be more like the relationship between business and consumer (Moe 1994). And as can be seen by the rights he took away from formerly incarcerated individuals as well as the implicit right to welfare he took away in transforming AFDC, he arguably did more than Reagan in emphasizing citizen responsibilities over citizen rights, and more than Reagan in emphasizing the punitive arm of government. However, in part because he appointed more African American appointees than anyone before him, and expressed a significant level of comfortability with black people—so much so that some jokingly referred to him as the country's first "black president"—he escaped significant criticism.

Under the neoliberal turn, cities and individuals alike are forced to become more and more entrepreneurial, bearing both the responsibility and the risk for a range of actions. Under the neoliberal turn, progressive policies like welfare, public housing, and unemployment insurance are either slashed or are attacked, as these policies are viewed to make people *less* entrepreneurial and less responsible for their own choices. Although the drug gangs that quickly fill the vacuum left by manufacturers do generate a certain type of "entrepreneur"—the hustler represented by Ace Hood—that particular entrepreneur is routinely victimized and punished by the government. Further, as federal and state governments reduce local governments' ability to collect tax revenue, cities themselves are forced to become more "competitive" by remaking themselves for the purposes of capital.

Along these lines, I noted the importance of the Financial Control Board in disciplining New York City, forcing it to stop providing a range of services for city residents.

Truth be told, though, cities do not reduce *all* of their services. In fact, some services increase. In order to entice downtown business development, cities increasingly provide a range of services to corporations and real estate developers, often giving them help with drafting development proposals, and giving them a range of tax write-offs that enable them to purchase and develop land inexpensively. Cities increasingly devote resources to transform themselves into tourist hubs.[12]

---

12   Take Times Square. Almost 40 million people visit Times Square every year. It bombards the senses with brilliant high-resolution billboards ten stories tall, a cacophony of car horns, movie trailer soundtracks, street musicians, cellphone conversations, and clicking camera shutters.

But thirty years ago Times Square was home to perhaps the most vibrant pornography film district in the nation. It was a place for outcasts—the homeless, the indigent, the wayward, the sex worker. In a number of cities we see a subtle increase in a range of policies

I've noted how the central byproduct of neoliberalism is inequality. With the neoliberal turn, inequality within cities and inequality between cities increases. I've also noted that race plays a central role in the turn.

Chocolate cities — cities with large black populations — are the byproduct of particular social and political forces. As a result of defense policy, cities with significant industrial capacity hollow out, leaving poorer and blacker populations behind. As a result of civil rights legislation these populations have increased political power. As a result, we see the increased election of black political representatives. However, we also see three different political moves. While black political officials tend to be anti-racist, taking hard lines against racial discrimination, we see them mirror the rhetoric of their white counterparts when it comes to issues of poverty and crime. As a result of the forces that hollow them out, we see the cities themselves besieged by crises. Finally, when these crises occur, we see neoliberal solutions proposed to deal with them, making them worse.

* * *

and design elements that work to exclude undesirable populations. Park and subway car benches are increasingly designed to be homeless-proof and cities are increasingly passing anti-homeless regulations. Skateboarders are implicitly shunted away from downtown areas through the use of anti-skateboard handrails as well as through legislation.

In the case of Times Square a succession of mayors and political officials from Ed Koch to the city's first black mayor David Dinkins, to Rudy Guiliani, to Michael Bloomberg, supported zoning laws making pornography illegal within 500 feet of homes, schools, and churches. They aggressively enforced (illegal) anti-loitering laws, and developed rigid street vendor quotas (Barry 1995; Hicks 1994). Further, Giuliani cut development deals with Disney and other multimedia corporations to redevelop the area. While I do not want to make the provocative argument that a vibrant pornography industry was better for Times Square and New York City than the vibrant multi-neoned monstrosity we now have, I do want to suggest that Times Square thirty years ago was arguably a more public and open space than it is now, and that in transitioning Times Square to the disneyfied thing that we know now, public officials made an explicit decision to transform the space for the sole purpose of commerce.

> We have an obligation to give back. We have an obliga-
> tion to protect our women, our children, our elderly.
> —Former Philadelphia Police Chief
> Sylvester Johnson (Associated Press 2007)

> Teens need to make better decisions. Parents need to
> step up and take care of their children. We, as a govern-
> ment, cannot raise people's children. You want to have
> children? You have to take care of them.
> —Philadelphia Mayor Michael Nutter
> (CNN Wire Staff 2011)

Philadelphia is one of the nation's largest predominantly black cities. For more than twenty years the Pennsylvania Intergovernmental Cooperation Authority (PICA), an unelected body, has had significant oversight over the City of Philadelphia's finances. In order to be able to gain full access to municipal revenue, the city must submit (for PICA approval) a financial plan that ensures a balanced budget and access to short- and long-term credit markets. In the event of a previous shortfall, the financial plan must detail how that shortfall will be erased. The most recent big-ticket item PICA approved was the sale of Philadelphia's gas utility (Vargas 2014).

Like the example of New York City before it, PICA significantly shapes the political agenda of the city, its elected officials, and its political appointees. The two quotes above show how this plays out in official rhetoric.

By September 2007, Philadelphia made national headlines after almost 300 homicides had been committed. After a particularly rough stretch in which 27 murders occurred in a very short period of time, outgoing Philadelphia (African American) police chief Sylvester Johnson made what some deemed to be a radical call for 10,000 black men to patrol Philadelphia neighborhoods. The men would not be armed, would not be paid, would not be deputized to make arrests, but they would be trained in conflict resolution techniques. Johnson made his pitch to a number of prominent black male organizations, had the support of Dennis Muhammad (a former Nation of Islam official), and held a public recruiting event less than a month after he made his call. Before the year's end, close to 100 more men (and seven women) would be murdered, bringing Philadelphia's total to 392, the second highest murder total in almost ten years (Associated Press 2007).

Less than four years later, violent crime again brings Philadelphia into the national spotlight. After a series of (black) flash mob[13] assaults in two Philadelphia neighborhoods, Mayor Michael Nutter extended curfew hours for teenagers in the two neighborhoods hardest hit and increased the fines individuals guilty of violating curfew would have to pay. He then gave a blistering sermon at his (predominantly black) church, Mount Carmel Baptist, arguing the participants "damaged" their race. The events Nutter spoke to came at a particularly ironic time—less than two weeks earlier, an organization of Philadelphia youth (the Philly Youth Poetry Movement) took first prize in a prestigious San Francisco poetry contest and the youth (who'd done everything right and come from working class backgrounds themselves) felt as if they were overshadowed (CNN Wire Staff 2011).

In both examples, we see black political officials attempt to place primary responsibility for crime on black families. For Johnson, the primary responsibility fell on black middle- and upper-income men—the type of men W.E.B. Du Bois likely had in mind when he wrote about "the Talented Tenth" well over 100 years ago. For Nutter, the primary responsibility fell on black lower income families—the type of families Du Bois examined in *The Philadelphia Negro*. Once they articulate the problem of crime as a cultural problem, the solution becomes clear. For Johnson, if black males don't have the right role models, if they are culturally predisposed to dislike and distrust the police, then they need to be exposed to black men who care about them, and these black men need to replace the police.

There are a range of other drastic measures Johnson could have pursued, particularly because he was on the cusp of retiring. He could have, for instance, implored the city to legalize drugs or to stop prosecuting non-violent drug crimes. He could have attempted to do what the character of Sergeant Bunny Colvin did in the Baltimore drama *The Wire*—render

---

13 Large groups of individuals quickly mobilized by social media.

certain areas of the city drug-enforcement free. But he didn't. Instead, he suggests black men engage in a partnership with the city that would have them take on almost all of the risk and many of the responsibilities of police officers, without any of the training, the equipment, the legal protections, and the pay and benefits. And, of course, they are expected to do this while working on their jobs and being good husbands, fathers, etc.

It's not hard to see the problems here. What would happen if a citizen ended up suing one of Johnson's "volunteers"? When citizens sue the police for violating their rights, police officers are protected and defended by the state. Would the volunteer pay for his own defense even though he's performing the police officers' job? On the flip side, what recourse do citizens have if one of the volunteers commits an act of brutality? Johnson's solution to crime remakes black families into extra police units, placing much of the responsibility for policing, a responsibility black citizens pay taxes for, on the backs of black citizens and families themselves. But because the citizens under discussion are black, the idea seems like common sense.

Black people wisely passed on Johnson's suggestion. However, it is noteworthy that no one, to my knowledge, publicly raised these critiques of the program.

For Nutter, if black families don't have the capacity to raise their kids, then to the extent the government should be involved, it should be involved in punitively forcing families to *develop* the capacity. To the extent the government has any responsibility at all here, it is to *force* responsibility onto black parents. I mentioned PICA above. Philadelphia continues to face a budget crisis. Parks and Recreation had its budget cut to the tune of $8 million in 2013. In fact, over a five-year period, the department received $43 million less than the FY 2009–2013 budget promised. Furthermore, when political officials decided to increase the city parking lot tax, they promised (but never gave) a portion of that money to the department (Greco 2012). These budget cuts kept Parks and Rec from providing the full suite of youth programs and routine maintenance it normally would. As a result of the cuts in maintenance, a Philadelphia neighborhood group had to raise money themselves for a broken slide, spending $600 of their own money (Greco 2012).

While Nutter referred to the economy in his sermon about the flash mobs, stating that he understood how it negatively affected neighborhoods, he made no mention of the role budget cuts played, no mention at all of how the city's Parks and Rec's budget had been slashed.

We can imagine what his sermon could have looked like if he had. If he explicitly tied the flash mobs to lack of youth activities and then to the slashed budget, he could have theoretically used his sermon to urge city stakeholders to accept tax increases that would lead to better services. Nutter made little mention of the lack of youth employment opportunities, even though he noted how hard hit the families of those neighborhoods were because of the depression. Again, we can imagine what his sermon would have sounded like if he had—Philadelphia is one of the most important economic hubs on the east coast, second only to New York City. If Nutter would have focused on the lack of youth jobs, we could imagine him using the opportunity to urge churchgoers and other listeners to push the development of job programs at the local, state, and federal levels. Here, given the role construction still plays in cities like Philadelphia Nutter could have called for more youth construction jobs. Particularly, given problems with the School District of Philadelphia (which, in another example of the slow death of local political power, was taken over in 2001 by the Pennsylvania governor), one could imagine using such a push to deal with two problems at once. He could have easily taken the angst those parents feel and transformed it into a call for more municipal resources. But when he did call for more resources, he called for more resources to punish and surveil seemingly "irresponsible" working class black families, increasing curfew hours and increasing the fine for violating curfew hours, *but only in those neighborhoods.* He was all for spending more resources on neighborhoods when it came to spending money on police enforcement. Instead of saying these neighborhoods have more problems and require more political and economic resources, he was, in effect, saying that these neighborhoods have more problems and require *more policing.*

Johnson implicitly attributed the spread of crime to the lack of black role modeling and the lack of black policing. For him, it was a cultural issue tied to black-on-black crime. For Nutter, too, the problem was a cultural one and one primarily about black familial responsibility in a narrow sense and in a broader sense. In the narrow sense, he explicitly noted that government had *no* responsibility for raising children. Rather, it was the family's responsibility. Taking his sermon along with the anecdote above about the $600 slide — the one the neighborhood had to raise money to pay for — we can see him pushing more and more responsibility down to the families themselves, virtually crushing them. And, as he pushes more and more responsibility down on them, he, like Johnson, increases the scale and scope of *their* responsibility. Nutter makes the speech in a predominantly black church because the issue again is not primarily a political one but a cultural one. If it were a political issue he would've spoken at city hall. If it were an economic issue he would have spoken in the center of Philadelphia's business district. But because he represented the issue as primarily a moral and spiritual one unique to black populations, he gives a speech at a predominantly black church. And because the issue is primarily one of twofold black irresponsibility — the black children were being irresponsible in embarrassing the race, black parents were being irresponsible in raising those children — he explicitly speaks to and punishes black communities.

Now, one argument we could make about Nutter and Johnson is that neither have love for black folk. And that both have, in effect, "sold out". But this argument doesn't really work. Nutter didn't just give his sermon in a black church — to considerable black applause — he did so in his *own* church. Nutter could even be said to have love for hip-hop. Not only was he a DJ in his younger days, he performed Rapper's Delight (the ten-minute extended version) at one of his inaugural events, backed up by Questlove (DJ of the Philly-based hip-hop band The Roots). Similarly, Johnson had support from a former member of the Nation of Islam, suggesting that he had support for his idea from at least a portion of Philadelphia's black nationalist community.

Instead, we can make an argument that Nutter and Johnson were both able to use their love for black people to actually *bolster* their neoliberal rhetoric. Nutter couldn't have made this clearer. The poor and working class black kids involved in the flash mobs were not only "representing" themselves, they were representing *the entire black community*. As such, *they*—not the state, not the city, not the political officials in charge of the city—are responsible to change their behavior. Without the state resources required to do so.

These two examples reveal the unique problems black elected officials pose for black citizens in the wake of the neo-liberal turn. Neither could be said to dislike black people or black culture. But even as their cultural roots connected them to their communities in certain ways, it also gave them the latitude to criticize their black constituencies in ways their white counterparts arguably couldn't.

The neoliberal turn doesn't happen without crisis. I referred to the example of New York City above—the austerity program forced on New York City was not possible without the fiscal crisis the city faced in the seventies. Currently, New Orleans and Detroit (two of the nation's most prominent chocolate cities) represent the "best" twenty-first-century American examples of the function crisis performs in cities. Hurricane Katrina struck the Gulf Coast in 2005 and was one of the most costly disasters in American history, taking over 1800 lives and causing almost $110 billion in damages. Over the past several decades Detroit lost almost two-thirds of its population and hundreds of millions of dollars in municipal revenue as a result. At the height of the twenty-first-century depression approximately 50% of Detroit's workforce was unemployed (Wilkinson 2009). In March 2013 Michigan governor Tom Snyder (GOP) placed the City of Detroit under emergency financial management, giving almost all of the power of its elected representatives to an unelected emergency financial manager. A little over a year later that manager (Kevyn Orr) filed for bankruptcy, the largest such filing in American history.

I used the two Philadelphia examples above to show how black political officials dealt with black populations deemed to be problematic. What we see in the cases of New Orleans and Detroit are more akin to system-wide neoliberal makeovers. Public housing in New Orleans has not only served to provide inexpensive housing to New Orleans's poor working-class community, it has also served as a valuable space of community building and political activism. In the wake of Katrina, political and economic elites used the disaster to attempt to gut public housing. Rather than handle the rebuilding project directly, the federal government subcontracted almost all of the disaster and recovery projects to private corporations. The end result? Most of the monies allocated to help New Orleans rebuild ended up going to corporations in the form of profit, and many residents ended up being saddled with more debt than they had before the hurricane hit.

Detroit wasn't hit by a Class 5 hurricane, but the effect of private and public disinvestment was no less severe. As a result of a combination of a diminishing tax base, a series of giveaways to corporate investors, and a bond deal so skewed it won an award from a national bond buyers' organization,[14] the city

---

14   Kwame Kilpatrick is now viewed as the poster child for bad urban government, as Kilpatrick is currently serving a 28-year sentence for corruption. As a mayor and as a state representative (before elected mayor, Kilpatrick served as a state legislator) Kilpatrick consistently used his office to enrich his friends and his allies at the expense of the (black) taxpayers he represented. However, for my interests, perhaps the most important crime Kilpatrick committed may not have technically been a crime. In 2005 the city (under Kilpatrick's leadership) borrowed approximately $1.5 billion in variable-rate debt in order to cover the costs of taking care of retired Detroit workers, a deal that was the city equivalent of the adjustable-rate mortgage loans that led to the financial crisis of 2008.

> The deal involved two layers of speculative financial instruments. One layer involved "pension obligation certificates of participation"—essentially IOUs that allowed Detroit to borrow money to give to its two pension funds.
> The second layer involved interest rate swaps, a high-risk bet that Detroit lost. The certificates of participation carried a variable interest rate. So the city bought the swaps as a hedge against the risk that interest rates would rise. In fact, interest rates fell sharply during the 2008–2009 financial crisis. The city lost the bet, adding to the pensions' underfunding by as much as $770 million over the next 22 years.
> Under the terms of the swap contracts, the banks were owed up to $400 million in early 2009 when the city's credit rating fell below investment-grade status. (Bomey 2013)

Since 2002 *The Bond Buyer* (a municipal finance publication) has recognized innovation in municipal finance at an annual gala. In 2005 Kilpatrick was one of the awardees.

Kilpatrick was sent to prison in part for extorting approximately $850,000. The deal Kilpatrick was awarded for cost the city almost 40 times more in real money, but arguably more than that in political terms.

was placed under emergency financial management. One of the reasons Detroit became important in the first place was because it is situated near the largest body of fresh water on the planet. To deal with the city's budget crisis, the city's water department slashed its employment rolls by over 1500 workers, increased its water bills over 100% over a ten-year period, and in 2014 sent shut-off notices to almost 50,000 residents (Kaffer 2012, Smith 1999). Some estimate that 40% of the city's 88,000 street lights are inoperable (Helms et al. 2014). In January of 2015 a story about a 56-year-old Detroiter (James Robertson) who had to walk over 21 miles to work went viral (Laitner 2015). His commute was so tortuous because the metropolitan Detroit region's public transportation system is poorly integrated and resourced. Its bond ratings as of 2012 were *five levels below investment grade* (Preston and Christoff 2013). Detroiters weren't asked to equally share its burden, however. Mike Illitch, owner of the Detroit Red Wings (and the Detroit Tigers), was given almost $290 million in public resources to build a new $450 million stadium for the team in the heart of the city (Bradley 2014).

Public policy was largely responsible for the growth of both Detroit's and New Orleans's metropolitan region. Public policy was also responsible for their fall. In Detroit's case, the fall comes from the government-subsidized creation of racially exclusive suburbs on the one hand, and government-subsidized decentralization of big business on the other. In the case of New Orleans, the fall comes from the failure of the government subsidized canals.[15] Now, even given the fact that the problems both cities face come from public policy in the service of private interests, public policies could still have protected the cities from the calamities they faced.

In the case of Detroit, a regional solution could have spread out the impact of the exodus of auto manufacturers in a way that would have protected the region in general and Detroit specifically. Alternatively, the leadership of Detroit could have

---

15 Here William Freudenburg's (2009) work on Katrina is required reading. The marshland that would have conceivably protected New Orleans from even a class 5 hurricane like Katrina was destroyed by the Mississippi River Gulf Outlet (MRGO) — a canal built by the Army Corps of Engineers but pushed by local business interests.

either increased taxes, perhaps kept taxes stable, or even pursued such radical strategies as buying teams like the Detroit Red Wings themselves.

In the case of New Orleans the Federal Emergency Management Association (FEMA) could have been far more effective in managing Katrina even after it happened. Rather than creating a plan that assumed New Orleans residents could and should be responsible for their own transportation they could have created a plan that took better advantage of existing transportation resources to take care of a higher percentage of their citizenry.

The fact that both cities were and are still "chocolate cities" significantly increased the degree to which people inside and outside of the region tended to think both cities were ungovernable. As New Orleans and Detroit's population became (and was increasingly depicted as) poorer and blacker, the attitudes of whites became more and more antagonistic. Ever since Detroit's been run by black elected officials it's been castigated in the media and by political officials as being uniquely corrupt. New Orleans has historically been promoted as being one of the most corrupt cities in the nation. Similarly, big government itself has been proposed as being corrupt as well and, at the very least, inefficient. When Katrina hit New Orleans, and when Detroit's fiscal straits became clear, the last thing people wanted to think about was the potential that government could actually *solve* the problems the cities faced.

This doesn't mean that progressive forces simply left the cities to die. Far from it. However, to the extent each city had a reservoir of goodwill because of their unique histories—Detroit's status as the capital of the modern industrial age, and New Orleans's status as the jazz capital of the world—a range of populations and non-government institutions were mobilized to come to their aid. Even the aid they received, though—which primarily comes in the form of "social entrepreneurship"—is neoliberal in nature.

In New Orleans, for example, the organization Go Propeller has incubated an organization that's successfully raised over $20,000 to help clean up the 2010 BP oil spill, a legal center that's helped more than 1500 clients with non-violent criminal records find work, and another legal center that's successfully won approximately $300,000 in benefits for disabled children.[16] Detroit boasts similar projects, from for-profit firms like the Fresh Corner Café (which provides inexpensive fresh food to food deserts), Rebel Nell, which employs working-class Detroit women to make graffiti-inspired jewelry, non-profit firms like The Empowerment Plan, which hires homeless residents to manufacture coats that double as sleeping bags, and Motor City Blight Busters, which works to help demolish tens of thousands of abandoned homes. And in the cases of both the water-shutoff and James Robertson, volunteers were swiftly mobilized to help pay the water bills of those threatened with shutoffs, and to help purchase James Robertson an automobile.

Finally, in both cases we see a significant increase in the numbers of young entrepreneurial members of "the creative class" — predominantly white educated artists, intellectuals, and small business owners interested in taking the opportunity of cheap real estate and relatively open space to take the types of economic risks that would be almost impossible in cities like New York City or San Francisco.[17]

The entire concept of social entrepreneurship relies upon the notion that innovation, creativity, and energy are best mobilized by the application of market principles, particularly in crisis cases like Detroit and New Orleans. It misses the crucial role business principles played in generating the crisis, and the role government should play in solving the crisis. Robinson isn't the only person with such a long commute to work, but pitching him as if he were masks the deep systemic challenges that led to his transportation problem in the first place. He commutes from the city because manufacturers fled as a partial byproduct of legislation designed to make it easier for them to do so. There are few reasonable public transportation options because automobile manufacturers conspired to make a particular individualistic vision of freedom (captured by the

---

16 All information taken from the Go Propeller Impact page (gopropeller. org/impact).

17 The works of Cedric Johnson (2011) and Jay Arena (2012) are particularly important in unpacking the neoliberalization of New Orleans.

idea that every individual should own a car and have the free-dom to go where he/she wanted) universal,[18] and because the (predominantly white) suburban residents don't want to subsi-dize the transportation costs of poor and working class (black) Detroit residents.[19] The BP Oil Spill of 2010 was one of the great-est environmental catastrophes of the nascent twenty-first century. While any effort to deal with the problems of the oil spill should be applauded, even a cursory cost of the cleanup (which affected more than 15,000 miles of coastline) runs into the *billions*. There is no amount of individual charity that could effectively generate the infrastructure needed to clean up the spill.

In the sixties Henri Lefebvre argued that the central battle of the latter decades of the twentieth century would be the battle over the city, the battle over the "right" to the city. Who should have the ability to determine how the city functioned, the people who lived, worked, and played in the city, or the people who "owned" it? While Lefebvre's work was far-sighted, he totally ignored the fundamental role race and racism would play in that battle. Around the same time Grace and James Boggs believed that the city was the black man's land, and that cities like Detroit should become revolutionary black polit-ical strongholds from which new visions of urban life could develop. Unlike Lefebvre, they did understand the role race and racism played, but by the mid-seventies they'd moved

---

18 Compare this vision, for example, to a vision of freedom that posited that metropolitan areas should be integrated such that individuals without vehicles wouldn't need them to move around.

19 This, combined with the fear of giving poor blacks easy access to white suburbs. This is not a uniquely Detroit problem. In 2014, for example, the Atlanta region was hit with one of the worst snow storms in its history. In a Katrina-like snafu, rather than staggering school and work closings so as to give adequate time and room for commuters to pick up their children and get home, officials closed the schools without giving commuters notice, and then shut down the city at once. Because Atlanta suburbs have consistently turned down opportuni-ties to integrate the Atlanta region's public transportation system — in part due to racial animus — Atlanta commuters were stuck in traffic so long that in several cases the schools had to keep children overnight (Thompson 2014). One of my childhood friends moved to Atlanta from Detroit and was stuck in the storm so long she had to spend the night at a co-worker's home.

away from their position, because they saw the beginnings of the neoliberal turn in black-led cities firsthand. While the neoliberal turn has spread far beyond chocolate cities, the focus on the hustle is particularly prevalent within them. Black elected officials, rather than knocking the hustle — the legal hustle, at any rate — condemn their populations for not doing it enough, blaming a range of government issues on them. Similarly, we see this approach not only applied to populations within cities but, in the case of chocolate cities like Detroit and New Orleans, we see this applied to the cities themselves. Even solutions touted as progressive rely on the hustle for their energy. The city will likely remain ground zero for the battle against the neoliberal turn. But in that battle we'd do well to fight against the move to cast this solely as a fight against racism, as we will likely have to fight black elites with their specific black interests as well.

3

WHEN THE ECONOMY CRASHED IN 2008, AMERICA'S LARGEST automakers (Ford, General Motors, and Chrysler) lost so much money that two of them (General Motors and Chrysler) filed for Chapter 11 bankruptcy and were briefly taken over (GM by the federal government, Chrysler by the UAW and Fiat). The entire world felt the brunt of the crash, but, as I implied in the last chapter, Detroit was arguably hit harder than any other major American city. On December 7, 2008, while Congress debated whether to bail the automakers out, a *New York Times* journalist wrote an article ("Detroit Churches Pray for God's Bailout") about a special service held in one of Detroit's most prominent megachurches, Greater Grace Temple (Bunkley 2008). Bishop Ellis conducted the service for the hundreds of churchgoers directly or indirectly employed by the auto industry. He wasn't the only one—several Detroit area Catholic churches had similar services, dedicated to getting their worshippers through the auto industry's trying times.

But his service was perhaps the most audacious in its attempt to bring God into the fray.

The article's feature photograph depicts Greater Grace's leader, Bishop Charles H. Ellis III, waving his hands furiously on an elevated stage (backed by his choir) while a liturgical dancer performs in the center aisle.

On the stage, between Bishop Ellis and the choir, were three sparkling white Cadillac Escalades.

Why the Escalade? The Escalade, one of General Motors' most expensive vehicles, symbolically stands in for the twofold aspirations of churchgoers. People who work for GM depend on the Escalade (and other cars like it) for their livelihood. People who don't work for GM but believe in the American idea of upward mobility see the Escalade as representing that vision. Perhaps they can't afford an Escalade *now* but, if they put the effort in, they will be able to afford an Escalade at some point in the near future.

I'd also suggest that the Escalade served as a stand-in for the city of Detroit itself, simultaneously representing Detroit's storied past—when it was known as the Paris of the West—and its desired future.

The *New York Times* journalist revisited Greater Grace a year and a half later, this time focusing on Marvin Powell, a middle-aged Pontiac Assembly plant autoworker and one of Greater Grace's armor bearers.[1] A family man much like my father, the autoworker and his wife had two small children and a $150,000 mortgage. One of the few people in the region still able to make a good living without a college education (he attended college but withdrew for financial reasons), Powell was on the cusp of being let go, as the plant was in danger of being shut down. Given his age and the lack of a college degree, his job prospects in the event of being let go looked bleak. I was struck by the following quote:

> Powell is a popular figure at Pontiac Assembly. Some of his co-workers have encouraged him to run for office at their local, and people often ask him what he thinks is going to happen at the plant and what he intends to do if it closes. "No. 1, I tell them I can't worry about what I can't control; no matter what I say or do, I can't keep the plant open," Powell says. "And No. 2, I tell them that God provides for his own, and I am one of his own." (Mahler 2009)

This quote struck me for a few different reasons. Because Powell reminded me a lot of my own father (who worked dozens of six-day weeks over the course of three decades to provide for us), I immediately thought about how much better off Powell

---

1   An armor bearer is an honorary church position some churches bestow that designates an individual as the church leader's protector.

would have been if he'd been born in the forties or fifties rather than the late sixties or early seventies. Not only would he be looking at a good retirement, he'd likely have put his two children through school already.

I also thought about how resilient he had to have been to continue going to work and providing leadership for his church and his co-workers even in the face of a looming layoff.

Finally, I was struck by his leadership and his (lack of) politics. The position of armor bearer is a high honor normally bestowed upon the most dedicated worshippers and church leaders. Similarly, union members don't just ask anyone to run for office. However, his leadership traits do not translate into progressive politics. It doesn't occur to him, for example, that working with the union could potentially save both his job and the jobs of the co-workers he obviously cares about. In Powell's opinion, those who choose God will be saved from the worst of the economic crisis *while those who don't, won't.*

Around the same time the *New York Times* journalist visited Greater Grace, I visited a predominantly black church in Baltimore County. The pastor, like Bishop Ellis, was a powerful orator. And just like Ellis, the pastor routinely used the pulpit to speak to the economic crises afflicting black communities in general and his community specifically. Words cannot convey the powerful effect his sermon had on churchgoers. I saw men and women walk in the church burdened by fear, depression, and economic anxiety, and I saw them leave uplifted and prepared for battle.

But as uplifting as his message was for churchgoers, the content of this message was far from uplifting, because he believed all of the ills associated with the economic crisis (increased debt, poverty, unemployment, stress and anxiety, marital discord) were caused by a *poverty mindset.* This mindset affects individual habits — it causes people to spend money (perhaps on the latest Air Jordans) when they should save, it causes them to be late to work instead of being early, it causes them to lay around the house when they should be hustling. In a word, this mindset makes people *undisciplined.* And this mindset reflected and was caused by a poor relationship with God.

Note the logic here. People are materially poor because they don't think right. Their inability to think right makes it impossible for them to receive God's blessing.

These ideas were contained in a series of sermons sold as a CD package called "Destroying the Root of Debt".

> Now debt is a form of bondage. Now I don't want to spend a lot of time telling you how it binds you because most of you know that. It is a form of bondage. Limitation. Constraint. And Christ came to set us free from all forms of slavery. In order to enjoy our complete freedom in Christ and never be entangled with financial debt again we must attack it at its root....God hates debt. So he will miraculously provide favor, forgiveness and favor, everything you need to get out of debt but if you have not learned the discipline of living a debt-free life you will always go back and that's with anything in Christ Jesus....I'm coming to understand this more, a lot of time God opens doors for us and he will provide opportunities but if you don't discipline your flesh those opportunities will be lost, those doors will be closed. (Robinson 2008)

If people are materially poor because they are undisciplined and because they lack a personal relationship with God, then what's the solution?

They need to become disciplined in part *through* a personal relationship with God.

The connection he makes is one that neatly fits common sense about black populations—black people are poor or experience financial hardship not necessarily because of structural issues but because of personal failings. And it fits the common desires we all have for some degree of control over our circumstances.

The pastor of the church I visited is a disciple of Dr. Creflo Dollar, founder and senior pastor of World Changers Church International. Dr. Dollar regularly delivers sermons to over 30,000 at his church in Georgia, and to tens of thousands of others through satellite churches. Further, he delivers his message through a series of books including *No More Debt! God's*

Strategy for Debt Cancellation (Dollar 2000). Dr. Dollar, like the Baltimore County pastor, believes that both the New and Old Testaments provide the perfect template for living a prosperous life. But living this life requires understanding and acting on God's Word.

> Matthew 11:12 tells us that "... *the kingdom of heaven suffereth violence, and the violent take it by force.*" In other words, prosperity will not fall out of the sky and into your lap. There are biblical principles that must be applied to your situations and circumstances before you see the manifestation of debt release. And the only way to apply those principles is to first destroy old patterns of thinking and develop a new mindset concerning debt and prosperity. A renewed mind is an important key to debt release. (Dollar 2000, pp. 12–13)

Above, we see the same focus on the mindset we see in the Baltimore County pastor. But there's more. What does a "new mindset" look like? How would we know someone with a new mindset if we encountered her? For Dr. Dollar, someone with a "new mindset" has a different attitude about the relationship between labor, saving, and prosperity. Rather than believe that the money one makes through labor should be saved, and then both applied to debt and applied to savings, Dollar uses the Bible to argue that someone with a new mindset has a very different attitude about the relationship between these concepts.

> God's system is based on giving and receiving. Sounds like a strange way to get out of debt, doesn't it? Let me explain. God's system is the exact opposite of the world's system. The world tells you to hoard every penny you've got, while God tells you to give in order to get out of debt. The key is obedience to God in your giving.
>
> If you desire to get out of debt, it's absolutely vital that you learn to give under the direction of the Holy Spirit. In Luke 6:38, Jesus says to "give" so that "... *it shall be given into you; good measure, pressed down, and shaken together, and running over, shall men give into your bosom ...*" Take a look at the first part of this verse. "*Give*

and it shall be given unto you ... " Giving to others causes others to give to you. And whatever you give will be returned to you....

The way out of debt is through giving. Give to live, and then live to give. Take a look at Matthew 13:3. I call this the grandfather parable of them all, because if you can get a good understanding of this, you will probably understand just about everything in the Bible. It says, *"... Behold, a sower went forth to sow ..."* Now stop right there. A farmer has to sow if he wants a harvest. And just as he will never harvest a crop by hoarding his seed, neither will you get out of debt by hoarding your money....

This mindset is a problem for many Christians. They think it's okay to give every now and again, but to give all of the time ... no way! (Dollar 2000, pp. 27–29)

Above, Dr. Dollar takes the Parable of the Sower—a parable Jesus uses to tell his disciples about the effect of spreading the gospel on different populations using the analogy of a farmer spreading seed on different types of soil—to talk about the relationship between labor, debt, savings, and prosperity. The seed Jesus refers to is the message of the gospel. But for Dollar, the seed has more than one meaning. The seed is the message, yes, which is sown among the people. The sower here is the pastor or the minister who sows the message of the Gospel to different people in the hopes that the message will be received properly and multiply. The ground here can be thought of as the hearts and minds of potential churchgoers. However, the seed is also money, which is sown amongst potential recipients, for the purpose of generating a spiritual and material harvest. Here the ground is different potential institutions, most important of which is the church. One of the ways is through tithing—churchgoers are expected to donate ten percent of their earnings to the church. The tithe is an incredibly important tool. Many pastors and churchgoers referred to tithing as "sowing the seed".

I'll come back to this.

In 2013 Kelvin Boston (host of the PBS show "Moneywise"), Dennis Kimbro (author of *Think and Grow Rich*), and a host of other economic empowerment luminaries and church pastors conducted a multi-city economic empowerment summit called "Faith, Family, and Finance". The summit was pitched to the same population that routinely attended churches like the one I visited in Baltimore County, like Greater Grace Temple in Detroit. In the beginning of one of the promotional videos advertising the summit, Boston engages in a call-and-response with the audience:

BOSTON:	Turn to your neighbor and say "Neighbor"
CROWD:	Neighbor
BOSTON:	"I am ..."
CROWD:	I am
BOSTON:	"...a millionaire ..."
CROWD:	a millionaire
BOSTON:	"...in the making."
CROWD:	In the making
BOSTON:	Now you have to say it like you really really mean it this time, okay, "I am ..."
CROWD:	I am
BOSTON:	"...a millionaire ..."
CROWD:	a millionaire
BOSTON:	"...in the making."
CROWD:	In the making
BOSTON:	Now give yourself a round of applause.
(*Crowd applauds.*)	

(KBMoneywise 2013)

The call-and-response tactic employed here was an important component of the equation—if they said the phrase enough times they'd come to believe it. Once they came to believe it, they would do whatever necessary to achieve it. Again, mindset dictates circumstance.

For some scholars, black churches remain a viable source of black political development (Alex-Assensoh and Assensoh 2001; Calhoun-Brown 1996; Harris 1999; McDaniel 2008;

Owens 2007; Tucker-Worgs 2011). Others take strong exception to this viewpoint, arguing that black churches pacify rather than politicize black men and women (Reed Jr. 1986a). Though not going as far as the most intense critics of black churches, Eddie Glaude (2007) has gone as far as to provocatively argue that the black church is "dead".

Is he right?

Greater Grace is a good example of a "megachurch", defined as a church with more than 2,000 members on average (it has approximately 6,000 members). Megachurches, like other churches, exist primarily to serve the spiritual needs of its churchgoers. However, their raw size enables them to engage in activities other churches cannot. For example, Greater Grace has 34 separate ministries listed on its website (and notes over 200 more), including separate ministries for men, women, and children, ministries for new members, ministries for ministers in training, ministries for people suffering from cancer and other life-threatening illnesses, ministries for media production and for information technology (the church's services look as if they were professionally produced and are regularly streamed over the Internet), among other things. The church site itself is so large it looks more like the headquarters of a multinational corporation than a place of worship.

Like traditional churches, megachurch members engage in volunteer projects. However, again because of their size, many megachurches conduct this work through community development corporations they own and operate. A 2007 *Crain's Detroit Business* article about Detroit megachurches noted almost $230 million in investments, including almost 230 single family homes and condominiums, two apartment complexes totaling over 200 units, and several banquet facilities and retail centers. The following passage captures the ethic espoused by megachurch pastors in general, and Greater Grace's pastor specifically:

> Church pastors often think of their neighborhoods as small cities, said the Rev. Charles Ellis III, pastor of the $36 million Greater Grace Temple on the city's northwest side. "What we're creating is a campus which we call the

city of David. When we built this church, we thought of
it being a city that would offer all kinds of activities."
Greater Grace's 20-acre "city" includes a banquet and
conference facility, retail centers, an 89-unit apartment
complex for senior citizens, a Montessori School and the
historic Rogell Golf Course, purchased from the city of
Detroit for $2.1 million in the spring. (Benedetti 2014)

Community development corporations have become such a
standard component of megachurch activity that one of the
pastors (Rev. Charles G. Adams, pastor of Hartford Memorial
Baptist) partnered with Harvard University to create a summer
workshop for pastors interested in starting their own CDCs
(Benedetti 2014).

The church I visited in Baltimore county was not a megachurch, though the pastor and many of its members desired
that it become one. The sermon I quoted from that church's
pastor, as well as the text I cited from Dr. Dollar, reflect "the
prosperity gospel" at work. We can see elements of it in both
the special Greater Grace Detroit service and in the Boston–
Kimbro "Faith, Family, and Finance" empowerment workshop.
Proponents of the prosperity gospel promote the idea that
people who follow the Bible will not only become spiritually
prosperous but will become materially prosperous as well. The
idea of using the Bible to become materially as well as spiritually prosperous may strike some as odd, given quotes in the
Bible that suggest that wealth and spiritual living do not go
together. Some Christians who believe too much wealth is a
sin, for example, routinely cite Matthew 19:24 ("Again, I tell you
it is easier for a camel to go through the eye of a needle than for
someone who is rich to enter the Kingdom of God"). Dollar and
other prosperity gospel ministers argue this quote and others
like it are misunderstood—it is not wealth but rather love of
wealth for its own sake that is the problem.

According to the inheritance package listed for us
in Deuteronomy Chapter 28, God promises to *bless*
or "empower to prosper" our baskets and store (v. 5). If
we were to translate that into today's language, *baskets*

would be our purses or wallets, and *store* would be our bank accounts, or the places we store money. Verse 8 tells us that the Lord will command His blessings on us. In verse 11, He promises to make us plenteous in goods....

However Deuteronomy is not the only place in the Bible that talks about prosperity. Psalm 35:27 informs us that the Lord takes pleasure in the prosperity of those who serve Him. And in Psalm 115:14, David let us know that we should expect to increase more and more.... Still you may be thinking, "Brother Dollar, that's the Old Testament! What does the New Testament have to say?" Third John [verse] 2 sums it all up for us. *"Beloved, I wish above all things that thou mayest prosper and be in health, even as thy soul prosperity."* You see, it is the will of God that we live a prosperous life. But no one can do that if they are broke. (Dollar 2000, pp. 60–61)

Many, though not all, megachurches are prosperity gospel churches.

Taking the work churches like Greater Grace increasingly perform in black communities in tandem with the prosperity gospel, we are left with a complicated picture. Certainly when Eddie Glaude argues that the black church is "dead" he is being purposely provocative. There's no way that we can say that a black church that invests tens of millions of dollars in revitalizing the black community it sits in is "dead".

Yet at the same time, we can certainly suggest that some of the ideas they promote about the relationship between black economics and black progress are, if not dead, then at least zombie-like. The data suggests, for example, that, contrary to the idea that blacks tend to spend frivolously, blacks are fairly frugal (Conley 1999). Contrary to the idea that blacks are broke because of spending habits, black financial troubles are driven by significant increases in the costs of education and housing rather than Xbox 360s (Ball 2014). Drilling down on specific segments of black communities, black college students have accrued a lot more debt in student loans than their white counterparts. In fact, they're more likely to drop out than white students *because* of their student loan debt (Kerby 2013). Several years before the housing market crashed the Department of Housing and Urban Development (HUD) found that almost 50% of home refinance loans in predominantly black Baltimore neighborhoods were subprime, compared to only 6% in predominantly white Baltimore neighborhoods (US Department of Housing and Urban Development Office of Policy Development and Research 2000).

This debt isn't accumulated because people spent too much time at the mall, or because they bought one car too many, or because they waited hours in line for the next pair of Air Jordans. Given the challenges Detroit, Baltimore, and cities like them face, one could argue that it makes a great deal of sense for churches like Greater Grace to think of themselves as miniature cities, because of their size (some larger megachurches are large enough to be considered cities), and because of the social services they increasingly provide for churchgoers and for their communities. However, one could also make the case that the trend towards megachurches and community development corporations is simultaneously a trend away from the types of grassroots activism that black churches are known for.

We are witnessing the neoliberalization of the black church.

However, this neoliberalization process is not alien to black communities. To a certain extent, what we're witnessing in churches like Greater Grace represents a resurgence of sorts. We can draw a straight line between early twentieth-century black-church behavior and contemporary black-megachurch behavior. Similarly, we can also draw a straight line from a range of church leaders who used their pulpit to preach a message of economic development to prosperity gospel proponents.

Take the role of black churches in the Great Migration. Black pastors recruited tens of thousands of black men and women to migrate North to work in the growing manufacturing sector. Their churches and organizations, like the Urban League, often worked with employers like Henry Ford to integrate black immigrants into Northern cities. As early as 1918 in Detroit, Ford granted black pastors like Second Baptist's Reverend Robert L. Bradby the power to recommend "good Negro workers" to the Ford employment office (Thomas 1992). In integrating them, black pastors emphasized "respectability". Black men and women in the North still had the capacity and the responsibility to carry themselves with dignity and distinction. Black elites hammered home this responsibility through sermons; they hammered this message home through pamphlets telling black men and women how to dress and how to parent. They hammered this message home through photographs depicting "respectable" black men and women. Ford employed this process to create a relatively integrated shop floor, but also to control labor quality.

Rev. Bradby and other leaders participated in this process because it gave them the ability to employ upstanding members of the growing Detroit black community (Dillard 1995; Meier and Rudwick 1979; Thomas 1992). But it also gave them significant social and political power. Second Baptist Church increased in both size and scope as a result of Bradby's activities—the more jobs he provided, the larger and more important his church became. And the larger his church became the more people he could serve and the more power he could accrue through serving them. Furthermore, the larger his church became the more activities the church engaged in. His church swiftly became one of the largest employee services in Detroit's black community.

Just as one could find forerunners of the megachurch in the early years of the twentieth century, we can find forerunners of the prosperity gospel there as well. In the early twentieth century, Phineas Parkhurst Quimby founded a religious movement called New Thought, which was based on the idea that individuals had the capacity to transform their reality through thinking. This movement had a number of different offshoots but they all contain the same germ of an idea, that thought transforms reality. Here, for example, is the Religious Science take:

> People initiate the...creative process at the level of Spirit by focusing on a thought or selecting an action to take. At the Soul level or in the Creative Medium, the thought is unconsciously subjected to the beliefs we

already hold personally or the beliefs we share with the race, resulting in the manifestation of our thoughts as we really believe them through the working of the Law. For example, if a particular woman wants a new job but feels lacking in her professional abilities and believes no one will hire her, or she believes that the job market is scarce, then her experience will be that she will not find a new job. In short, this teaching presupposes an intelligent and responsive universe.

Religious science seeks to teach a reliable system for creating positive life experiences. Its approach is to raise the consciousness of its adherents to a level of personal empowerment and responsibility grounded in the idea that human beings are created in the image and likeness of God even to the extent that individuals have the same creative power in the microcosm that God has in the macrocosm. It is taught that once this unity is recognized, the Universal Mind can be utilized by anyone to create a life abundant in health, wealth, and happiness. (Martin 2005, pp. 26-27)

E.W. Kenyon, an east coast pastor some view as the intellectual forefather of the Word of Faith movement, combined the central ideas of the New Thought Movement with Christian ideals and principles in the early years of the twentieth century. The first modern-day preacher to combine the use of mass media with a prosperity infused message was Oral Roberts. In the early fifties Roberts began broadcasting his citywide crusades on local television stations, within a short time developing a considerable broadcasting empire. Those early broadcasts included much of what we now associate with modern televangelism — demonstrative praise and worship, individualized healing (where the pastor would lay hands on and attempt to heal the ill), a sermon, and a call for financial assistance. Television airtime was expensive, and could not be provided for by crusade attendees alone. Roberts's solution was innovative.

> In order to subsidize the initial television pilots Roberts instituted an expanded financial partnership

> program referred to as the "Blessing Pact"…Persons were encouraged to send in money to the ministry according to their faith, and Roberts would pay for its tenfold return. Based upon the principles of seed time and harvest, Roberts professed that financial offerings are commensurate to sowing seeds. According to the natural order of God's law, believers will reap materially in tenfold proportion to what they sow materially by faith. (Walton 2006, pp. 85–86)

Oral Roberts was not the only pastor to promote this type of message. Over the last several decades a number of African-American pastors have promoted messages that strongly resemble those promoted by New Thought adherents, including Father Divine (founder of the Peace Mission), Reverend Ike (founder of the Christ United Church), and Daddy Grace (founder of the United House of Prayer) (Martin 2005). Modern-day proponents like Fred Price (head of Ever Increasing Faith Ministries), Ed Montgomery (head of Abundant Life Cathedral), and Creflo Dollar increasingly fuse high technology (sophisticated production studios, the Internet) with prosperity messages. The Baltimore County pastor I witnessed (a disciple of Creflo Dollar, himself a disciple of Word of Faith founder Kenneth Hagin) was not the first to use the Bible as a New Thought–inflected, spiritually based economic self-help tool.

I want to return briefly to the economic ideas I examined in the first chapter. Keynesian economists thought consumers were more important than producers and entrepreneurs because neither could profit if they had no consumers to buy their goods. Radical economists believed laborers were more important than business owners, because without laborers business owners would have nothing to sell. Neoliberal economists, on the other hand, thought entrepreneurs and business owners were more important than laborers or consumers, because if they didn't innovate, consumers wouldn't have jobs. Furthermore, society wouldn't progress. Keynesian economists thought governments should guide the economy in ways that would increase employment and productivity. Radical economists thought governments should guide the economy in ways that would improve human development. Neoliberal economists suggested these approaches would end up having the opposite effect.[2]

Here's where the idea of human capital comes into play. It transformed labor from a simple unchanging unit into something much more dynamic, something human beings could themselves transform through skill development, education, creativity, and *choice*. Just like a business owner spends money on research and development in order to increase productivity and profit, the new human being is supposed to spend the necessary capital to develop herself in order to increase her productivity and profit (defined in the individual case as income). Just like the market provides the business owner with the information needed to make rational assessments about risk so as to maximize his potential for profit (and reduce his potential for loss), the new human being is supposed to use the market to make rational assessments about how to develop herself to maximize her own profit-making potential. Finally, just like the market tends to reward businesses who make the proper risk assessment and develop themselves properly, and sanction businesses that don't, the woman who will not or cannot work and develop herself will tend to fail. Just like businesses that successfully develop their capital profit, and *should* profit according to capitalist common sense, individuals who successfully develop their *human capital* should profit according to neoliberal common sense.

Let me now connect this idea to the concept of sowing the seed, one of the central concepts of the prosperity gospel.

For Dollar and others, seed sowing is a form of human capital development. The act of graciously sowing the seed (the churchgoer is expected to not only give but to lovingly give[3]) represents an act of labor necessary for individual prosperity.

---

2   If laborers, for example, *knew* that they couldn't be fired, they would be more irresponsible. Their irresponsibility in turn would reduce their productivity, which would in turn make societies worse off rather than better off. If governments attempted to plan every aspect of the economy they would eventually fail and devolve into totalitarianism.

3   Here Dollar cites 2 Corinthians 9:7. The entire passage of the New International Version states: "Each of you should give what you have decided in your heart to give, not reluctantly, or under compulsion, for God loves a cheerful giver." Dollar takes the last portion, "...God loves a cheerful giver." (Dollar 2000, p. 30).

According to the prosperity gospel, the work the individual performs on himself in order to properly sow is the same work performed by the individual who figures out how to become more productive on the job or at school.

The prosperity gospel transforms the Christian Bible into an economic self-help guide people can use to develop their human capital. It transforms the impulse to become wealthy into a philanthropic impulse — prosperity gospel adherents do not want to become wealthy for the sake of being wealthy, they want to become wealthy in order to expand their capacity to do good deeds in the world. Along those same lines, the prosperity gospel transforms questions of wealth and poverty into questions of spiritual deservedness. Again the problem is that poor people have poor mindsets, poor habits, but also lack the proper spiritual anointing. It transforms risk assessment into faith assessment, which requires knowledge of God's true purpose, which is attained through prayer, through attending churches.

But also through the goods often sold by prosperity gospel pastors.

Many prosperity gospel churches contain stores selling their pastor's sermons and books, and also hold empowerment sessions. The church I visited weekly held such sessions for men and women providing a variety of materials (including economic workbooks) designed to help develop financial discipline and entrepreneurial activity in their members. After every sermon the pastor delivered, churchgoers were given the opportunity to purchase his sermon in CD form, giving them the ability to listen to the pastor at home, or on the way to work, or while working out. Additionally, he sold a debt relief package that included a workbook that helped individuals develop and balance their budgets.

The relationship between the churchgoer and the church (as well as the church pastor) is symbiotic. The churchgoer needs the church and the church pastor, but the church pastor needs the churchgoer. Dollar lists several components to sowing properly. I am going to focus on two, "Sow Into Good Ground" and "Give Expecting to Receive". Giving expecting to receive is a fundamental component of the prosperity gospel. As Dollar notes above, God expects Christians to be as materially prosperous as they should be spiritually prosperous. Christians should give and expect a return from their giving. But in order for that to happen the seed cannot just be sown willy-nilly, it has to be sown *in good ground*. How does Dollar define good ground?

> Malachi 3:8-10 makes it very clear that if you are not tithing, you are stealing from God. In light of all He has done and continues to do for you, ten percent of your income is not too much to ask. This is a small amount of seed that goes to managing His house — the church. In addition, the tithe is your covenant connector. It keeps the windows of heaven open over your life and activates the blessings and promises of God. You cannot expect supernatural debt cancellation if you refuse to obey God with your tithe.
>
> In addition, you cannot just tithe anywhere. You must be sure to sow your seed in a Word-based ministry that faithfully obeys God's instructions. (Dollar 2000, p. 76)

Later in the text, Dollar refers to the importance of developing a partnership with what he calls "the anointing", a godly power that operates through individuals, in this case through the right pastors. Indeed, Dollar goes as far as to note there is a "covenant relationship" that implies that the anointed has a responsibility to those he or she ministers to. Writing of his own responsibilities, Dollar notes that it is his responsibility to pray for God's blessings for his partners, to seek God on the behalf of his partners (who Dollar implicitly identifies as readers of his book), and to personally send letters as well as special gifts and tools to his partners. And in exchange his partners are responsible to pray for Dollar and his ministries and to support the ministry with tithes (Dollar 2000, pp. 101-2).

In other words, in exchange for tithes (and other support), anointed individuals directly contact God on the tither's behalf. Individual churchgoers choose between churches based on their ability to provide the type of information and the types of tools they need to properly develop their human capital, looking for the right place to "sow their seed", the way investors choose between stocks. Church leaders along these lines think of themselves as individuals selling themselves in order to sell God. In the wake of the neoliberal turn, black churches have increasingly become business-like institutions competing in the market. In 2014 Atlantablackstar.com published an article listing 8 black pastors around the world who make over 200 times more than their churchgoers. According to the article, Dollar is worth $27 million (Atlanta Black Star Staff 2014). The gap between these pastors and their churchgoers is very similar to the gap between corporate CEOs and their average workers. The CEO of General Electric, for example, makes 139 times more than its average worker, while the CEO of 21st Century Fox makes 268 times more (PayScale Staff 2014).[4] Which may help explain why in 2015 Dollar (briefly) asked 200,000 of his supporters to contribute $300 each to purchase a brand new jet—after a tremendous backlash, he rescinded the request.

The concept of prosperity as expressed in the prosperity gospel and its intellectual ancestors implies that there is enough resources to go around for *everyone* to be wealthy. The prosperity gospel can, if followed correctly, generate further prosperity for everyone. But this gospel ignores several aspects of labor. First, it ignores the structural conditions that modified labor in a way that made the possibility of shared prosperity remote. Second, it privileges spiritual work and discipline over physical labor. Third, it de-emphasizes labor solidarity over individual work. Fourth, even though it articulates shared prosperity, this shared prosperity acknowledges and to a certain extent depends on a significant wealth gap, particularly between church leaders and churchgoers.

Now, I recognize that in Detroit and other places like it there are pastors with more explicit progressive politics. In 2011, Baltimore's radical left caused Maryland Governor Martin O'Malley to halt a decision to build a $100 million jail for "youth charged as adults". This would not have happened without Pleasant Hope Baptist Church's Pastor Heber Brown

---

4   Although Dollar does not write about his personal worth in *No More Debt*, he does note that this gap is part of the deal, stating on page 105, "Of course [intercessors] get blessed. That comes with the territory" (Dollar 2000).

and other progressive black pastors.[5] Further, there are mega-churches with pastors who routinely connect black suffering to structural dynamics. But these churches are few and far between. Just as they were few and far between in places like early twentieth-century Detroit.[6]

The growth of the megachurch and the prosperity gospel represents the simultaneous neoliberalization of black churches and the return of black churches to the trajectory they were on before the intervention of the civil rights and black power movements. They represent remobilization projects that shunt black populations towards church development projects and personal discipline, rather than towards political organizing. At best this redirection reproduces the status quo and narrows the political imagination of individual churchgoers. At worst the prosperity gospel in particular generates an intense desire for personal growth that can only rarely be attained by the practices pastors propose. A desire that when unmet generates

5   In fact, Baltimore has a long history of progressive pastors. The founder of one of Baltimore's most storied black churches (Union Baptist) was present at the Niagara Movement (the forerunner of the NAACP) and its second leader (Reverend Vernon Dobson) created Baltimore's first Head Start program, ended city discrimination against black business, and founded BUILD (Baltimoreans United in Leadership Development—a predominantly black working-class community power organization) through his work with the "Goon Squad" (a group of black activists who led Baltimore's civil rights movement).

6   When Ford's exploitation of workers and his racial discrimination became painfully apparent, Reverend Bradby and other black leaders found themselves in a precarious position. They relied on Ford to dole out jobs in part because these jobs were primary sources of their church's prestige. It was difficult for them to generate sermons attacking Ford. It was difficult for them to provide organizing spaces for people to work against Ford. Churchgoers were constrained as well. The power pastors like Bradby often wielded could and often did make it difficult for churchgoers to give voice to different opinions and different sets of actions. And during those moments when they did decide they wanted to go against their pastor, they often had to contend not only with other churchgoers—who may not have felt similarly—they had to contend with the charismatic authority of the pastor himself. Black churches in places like Detroit took a more progressive route because they had to respond to the increased demand for black activism expressed by black churchgoers and mobilized by black progressive middle class pastors on the one hand and a combination of unions and national organizations like the NAACP on the other.

a more intense desire for the practices themselves, rather than critical resistance — because if churchgoers don't get the results they look for it has to be their fault, they must not be prayerful enough, disciplined enough. As banks became more and more profit-driven in the wake of the neoliberal turn, many of them have aggressively tried to make money on the poor using the guise of progressivism, arguing that serving the "unbanked" — men and women who, because of their poverty, perhaps in combination with their poor neighborhood, do not have access to traditional banking services — represents an "untapped market" that can be used to not only increase profit margins for the bank but provide a much needed service to the poor. In the growth of the megachurch and the prosperity gospel, we often see something very similar, with churches increasingly reaching out to the "unchurched", treating this population as if it too were an "untapped market". As both the people and the churches find themselves in dire economic straits, we need a new set of ideas as well as a new set of institutional practices in order to direct these churches towards more progressive ends.

4

ONE OF THE MOST IMPORTANT DEBATES BLACK INTELLECTUALS engaged in at the onset of the twentieth century concerned education. Should black people be given a classic liberal education, designed to pursue the good and just life, or should black people be given a vocational education, designed to give them the skills and discipline needed to become financially independent? W.E.B. Du Bois was the most prominent proponent of the former, Booker T. Washington was the most prominent proponent of the latter. The consequences of this debate for African Americans were significant—although evidence suggests that Washington may have privately supported black political activism, we know that publicly not only did he make a number of statements in support of Jim Crow, his model of education hurt black laborers and helped wealthy whites (Anderson 1988). But there were broader consequences for the rest of society—if the nation promoted Washington's ideas about education, America's schools would be transformed and the very purpose of education would be limited to giving Americans the skills they need to find jobs, as opposed to giving Americans the tools they need to become fully human.

In the current moment three overlapping crises loom large in discussions about the American education system. One crisis concerns the increasing threat posed by our competitors in the international economic arena. People concerned about this threat see America falling further and further behind India, China, Japan, and other nations, because our children are under-educated in comparison to their overseas peers. Domestically, a range of educators are increasingly concerned about the growing divide within the nation between black and Latino children and their white counterparts on the one hand,

and between children educated in urban school systems and children educated in suburban school systems on the other. Finally, people are increasingly concerned with the growing cost of education. On average, even after the recession, state support for state colleges like the University of Michigan have decreased approximately $2400, even as tuition in state colleges has *increased* approximately $1300 (Hiltonsmith and Draut 2014). Similarly, federal grant aid to students has been reduced, and student reliance on loans has increased.

In this chapter I address the neoliberalization of education. Increasingly, parents, students, teachers, principals, superintendents, schools, and school districts are expected to adhere to the values of the market, changing the purpose of education itself. And while this has broad effects given the particular role education plays in black communities, this move is particularly dire for them. The three crises I note above are all partially responsible for the growing neoliberal transformation of education, a transformation that itself generates its own crisis. And, like the transformation of the church, we see African Americans not simply victimized by this transformation but involved in its spread, as the reduction of democratic values that lie at the heart of the neoliberal transformation not only take political power away from black people, it reduces our political imagination to the point where it is difficult for us to even imagine a form of education that isn't solely about increasing one's preparedness for a *job*.

* * *

In 1983 Ronald Reagan's Secretary of Education created a national commission to study the state of America's educational system. Whereas Reagan wanted the Department of Education (created by his predecessor Jimmy Carter) abolished, the Secretary of Education had other ideas. The resulting report, entitled "A Nation at Risk", basically saved the Department of Education from destruction. Written when the country was in the middle of an economic depression, the report suggested that America's failing educational system was the result of America's failing economy. As a result of this report, states and local governments began to implement education policies based on the idea that the primary purpose of education was to train workers rather than prepare citizens.

By the time "A Nation at Risk" was published, it was clear that industrial cities like Detroit and Baltimore needed revitalization. Manufacturers had almost fully automated, and had not only fled the Rust Belt for the South and the West, they'd begun to flee the United States for foreign (cheap, non-unionized) labor. Left in the wake of the manufacturing exodus were schools primarily designed to prepare people for jobs in the manufacturing plants, jobs that no longer existed. City leaders wanted to attract businesses that could employ their citizens, and wanted to attract middle-class families that could help generate revenue and revitalize the city in other ways, but they felt they couldn't and believed the state of their school systems were to blame. Simultaneously, responding to the same forces to a certain extent, parents, teachers, and principals wanted more control over what happened in their schools.

As a result, city and state leaders began to promote four ideas. They promoted the idea of site-based management, giving parents, principals, and teachers in individual schools more authority in the hopes this would lead to better educational outcomes. In addition, they proposed taking over school systems themselves, placing school districts under the direct control of the mayor and the state governor. Now, it wasn't as if mayors didn't already have enough to do, particularly in the Rust Belt.[1]

But many mayors believed that they were being implicitly judged on the quality of their schools *anyway* and that they may as well actually take full responsibility for them. Furthermore, inasmuch as the businesses they were trying to attract not only wanted to be able to hire local graduates, they wanted

---

[1]   As they weren't flush with municipal revenue and couldn't go to either their state capital or to Washington, DC, to get resources, they had to consistently work to find ways to either pare down the services they *did* provide or they had to find alternative sources of revenue to provide the services they couldn't cut. This, while they had to also find new ways to attract businesses development. So one could argue that making mayors responsible for the schools was simply piling it on.

the middle-class families they relocated into the city to be able to have schools to place their kids in, mayors felt they had an extra responsibility. Finally, although many could and did argue that elected school boards were important vehicles with which taxpaying voters could exert some say in how their tax dollars were spent on education, the mayors believed that democracy was actually *failing* the school systems, in part *because* they relied on the popular vote. I'm going to come back to this later, but this is very important, because it suggests that the crisis of urban education is in part a crisis of *democracy*.

As a result, starting in 1989, state after state passed legislation giving state and local officials the power to permanently or temporarily take over failing school districts, "failing" defined either by persistent debt or by persistently high dropout rates. New Jersey, Kentucky, and four other states were the first to take over failing school districts in 1989. By 2004, more than 50% of states had taken over school districts, with the vast majority of these attempts occurring between 1995 and 1997 (Shober et al. 2006). And while some of these school districts were taken over for explicitly educational reasons, in the vast majority of cases school districts were taken over for fiscal reasons.

So the first two ideas were site-based management and school system takeovers. Third, state and local leaders proposed vouchers and charter schools. Educational vouchers are certificates of funding given to individual families that they can use in turn to spend on school tuition at participating public or private schools. Charter schools are public institutions; however, they differ from traditional public schools in that they receive a "charter" from the state to operate independently of the school district where they are geographically located. This charter gives them the flexibility to take students from inside and outside of their geographical area, as well as flexibility in hiring and in teaching. Between 1991 and 1999, 35 states passed charter school legislation.

Finally, state and local leaders proposed the increased use of standardized test scores in order to improve "accountability". In 1996 and 1999, the nation's governors convened at IBM's corporate headquarters. In both meetings, IBM CEO Louis Gerstner called for states to develop a standardized way to assess and measure educational outcomes in order to force schools to meet corporate expectations for their potential labor pool (Hursh 2001). Within a few years of their last meeting, the concept of standardized tests, already used to determine college admittances, had become the norm in most American states and, with the passage of No Child Left Behind, the nation itself.

Up to this point I'm putting a great deal of responsibility on political leaders at the state and local level. However, they weren't the only major players. Indeed, though federal, state, and local political leaders are important, venture philanthropists may be even more important, including foundations like the Lynde and Harry Bradley Foundation ($922 million in assets as of 2013), the Eli and Edythe Broad Foundation ($1.890 billion in assets as of 2013), the Bill & Melinda Gates Foundation ($41.310 billion in assets as of 2013), and the Walton Family Foundation of Walmart fame ($2.481 billion in assets as of 2013).

The move towards vouchers and charters, for example, comes in part from John E. Chubb and Terry M. Moe's (1990) *Politics, Markets, and America's Schools*. They argued that the central problem facing America's public school system was that it didn't give parents and students enough choice, and it didn't allow for enough competition. The Lynde and Harry Bradley Foundation provided significant funding support ($375,000) for their work, which transformed the conversation on American education. In 1989, two years after the school takeovers began, Wendy Kopp, a young Ivy League student, wrote an undergraduate thesis proposing the creation of a domestic peace corps of young teachers, who would go into the poorest school districts in rural and urban communities and transform them. The program she proposed became "Teach for America" (TFA). As opposed to the standard method of training teachers — sending them to educational school — TFA took students from a much wider disciplinary range in order to both increase the number of individuals interested in the teaching profession and lead to substantial innovation in the schools. From a first class of 500 idealistic kids, TFA now has over 8,000 teachers in schools and has over 32,000 alumni. The Eli and Edythe Broad Foundation is one of its largest supporters, giving over $10 million.

What do the phenomena I trace above have to do with the neoliberal turn?

The takeovers made possible by state legislation mostly occur in cities that have suffered the most from diminishing state and federal resources. The school systems in these cities are failing largely as a result of growing class and racial inequality, combined with those dwindling resources. The turn generates the conditions for failure and simultaneously uses those failures to call for more neoliberal solutions, in the form of better and more efficient "management", decreased democratic government, individual "choice" and "liberty", and vouchers and charters, which all supposedly give individual parents the freedom to look at a variety of options for their children alongside their neighborhood school. These modifications all come at a cost. Placing more responsibility on schools as opposed to dealing with the structural conditions they face tends to increase rather than decrease poor educational outcomes. As I show below, rarely have school takeovers either reduced debt or significantly improved educational outcomes.

The neoliberal turn itself doesn't come without a number of foundations and philanthropists promoting intellectual ideas. The venture philanthropists that promote charters, vouchers, new school district models, programs like Teach for America, and increasingly institutions designed to train and develop school officials, have driven the transformation of public schools into market-oriented institutions. Indeed, a quick glance at their funding programs reveal the stark use of market language in describing their philanthropy, as many of them focus on "investments" rather than "grants", on "ventures" rather than "programs", and on "social returns on investments" as opposed to "deliverables" (Scott 2009).

The shift towards charters and vouchers increasingly turns parents into private consumers. Traditional public schools situated in and based on local residence can serve a valuable community-building role. Indeed, the school often helps define the community. Similarly, the political organizations connected to the school—whether it be the PTA or the formal school board—can help develop community social and political capital. However, the move towards charters and vouchers significantly reduces that community-building potential. The parent is no longer situated in a community, but is rather a singular consumer interested in purchasing the best education for his or her child, in order to solely develop his/her human capital. To the extent democracy appears at all here, it appears in the form of "choice" and "freedom". Following up from this effect, the ability of communities to mobilize politically are destabilized because the number of neighborhood schools that can help cement those community ties are replaced by non-geographically bound charters.

The move towards charters in particular represents a wealth transfer from public to private sources. But this wealth transfer doesn't simply come in the form of for-profit management companies taking public resources. In 2000, Bill Clinton signed legislation authorizing "New Market Tax Credits". For Clinton and other more progressive neoliberals, the central problem poor neighborhoods faced was not capitalism itself, but rather the profound *lack* of capital. These tax credits would spur capital investments by making it far more profitable to invest in poor communities. Many of these tax credits ended up going towards the construction of charter schools (which were covered under the credits). Indeed, combined with other credits, investors could see as much as a 100% return on their investment within less than a decade, and as they're often loaning the money for charter school construction, this comes in addition to the interest they receive from the loan (Gonzalez 2010; Magliaro 2013). Many charters financed using these credits end up spending a significant portion of their revenue on debt service (as their rents have significantly increased) at the expense of education. Finally, as one of the ways charter schools reduce their costs is by hiring non-unionized teachers and staff, the charter schools indirectly reduce worker protections and reduce support for unions in general.

It's worth noting that many of the effects "competition" and "choice" (in the form of charters and vouchers) were supposed to introduce haven't occurred. Just as only a small portion of traditional public schools consistently produce excellent educational outcomes, only a small portion of charter schools do. The evidence suggests that charter schools on the whole either underperform their traditional public school counterparts or perform only as well as their traditional public school counterparts (Bifulco and Ladd 2006; Hanushek et al. 2007; Zimmer and Buddin 2006), that they may increase racial segregation (Garcia 2008), and rarely innovate in the class-room (Lubienski 2003), and that they are far harsher on their students than their traditional public school counterparts (Davis et al. 2015).[2]

Theoretically, the market is supposed to hold charters and vouchers accountable. But the education "market" doesn't quite function like this for many reasons, and I'll focus on three. First, because each school only has a limited number of posi-tions and award positions during a limited time period, parents end up being forced to compete with other parents, whereas if the market functioned "normally" each school would have as many positions as there was demand. As a result, schools are given much more power to choose, and much more power to shunt potentially problematic students away. Although the evidence suggests that most charters do not engage in "cream-ing"—that is to say, they do not use the power they have to accept only the best students—evidence does suggest that charters engage in "cropping"—that is to say, they may "crop off" their service in ways that end up underserving students with disabilities and special needs (Lacireno-Paquet et al. 2002). Further, inasmuch as some parents tend to have more resources than others, charter schools may end up providing more benefits for more resourceful parents.

Second, while theoretically "failing" schools should be punished by the market—parents aware that a given charter school is underperforming should stay away from that school, causing it to fail because of lack of students—the reality is quite different. The state of Michigan has the weakest charter school regulations in the country, in part because of the belief that the market would function better than any set of state reg-ulations. Rather than the "market" continually shutting down failing charter schools, the "market" allows poorly perform-ing charters to stay open year after year. Further, the "market" in the Michigan case allows charter schools—many of them operated by for-profit management companies—to keep their

---

books closed, preventing taxpayers from knowing how their money is spent (Dixon et al. 2014).

Third, bringing the profit motive into education is supposed to theoretically cause charter schools to innovate in order to do the best job of attracting "customers". But introducing the profit motive tends to have two other problematic effects. Particularly in the absence of regulations, it generates a perverse incentive to cut costs (which may cause charters to engage in the "crop-off" practice I note above). And it results in corruption, with charter school representatives receiving and doling out kickbacks for a variety of services (Dixon et al. 2014). Similarly, it ends up introducing a number of players in the education arena who are far more interested in profits than they are interested in education. An entire business sector has grown around charter school management. If we think of education, then, as not simply about educating, but also about a bundle of contracts (for construction, for management, for goods and services, etc.), we can see how much real money is at stake. Charter schools, then, are not simply about increasing support for the idea of market-oriented education, they are also about the money that goes into constructing and managing them.

Significantly increasing the number of quality teachers in the profession is a worthwhile endeavor, as is going against the market by putting our nation's best and brightest to work in some of our poorest urban and rural communities. However, in its attempt to transform education, TFA makes a few moves worth criticizing. First it explicitly supports de-regulating and to an extent de-professionalizing teaching by taking its teachers from a wide range of disciplinary backgrounds and suggesting that it's possible to fully prepare a graduate *without* a teaching degree for the rigors of a school classroom with little more than two years of on-the-ground training plus summer orientation sessions.[3] Second, it has been essential in the creation of a network of individuals and institutions dedicated to privatizing education. A number of its founders and

---

3   The research suggests that teachers recruited from TFA and other similar programs underperform their certified counterparts (Darling-Hammond et al. 2005; Kane et al. 2008; Laczko-Kerr and Berliner 2002).

its membership have either gone on to create individual charter schools, charter school organizations like the Knowledge Is Power Program (KIPP), charter school venture funds (New School Venture Fund), training programs (Broad Center for the Management of School Systems), and non-profits that promote charters; many have also taken leadership positions in federal, state, and local education endeavors. Indeed, arguably TFA has more influence in this sector than any other non-profit outside of the foundations from which it has received a significant portion of its resources (Kretchmar et al. 2014). And a number of them have run for office (Strauss 2013b). Just as charter schools and vouchers take money from public coffers for private purposes, generating a competiton over scarce resources that often leaves school systems poorer than they were before, TFA decreases city coffers through charging the cities the equivalent of a finder's fee for every TFA member they bring in, something cities wouldn't necessarily have to do for teachers hired through normal processes (Cohen 2015). Not only does this further reduce support for the idea that traditional teachers are valuable, given the financial straits many city school districts find themselves in, but the costs also end up taking a toll on city budgets — something that is particularly important to consider given the fact that TFA teachers don't out-perform their certified counterparts.

The changes I detail above generate the context for two of the most important pieces of education legislation passed since the sixties. One of President George W. Bush's most important domestic initiatives while in office was No Child Left Behind (NCLB), passed by Congress during his first year, a policy designed to take a "compassionate conservative" approach to education. NCLB created rigorous national standards (measured by performance on standardized tests) that schools, particularly those receiving Title I funds to educate poor populations, were expected to adhere to. Schools that showed a consistent pattern of underperformance would suffer a series of escalating sanctions, including being forced to pay for students to attend better-performing schools, and finally being shut down and having its entire staff replaced.

NCLB further attempts to transform the parent into the informed consumer. The legislation forces parents to use test scores to evaluate schools, and gives them the liberty and responsibility of choosing alternatives — especially charters and private schools — when the school doesn't deliver services effectively. The use of seemingly objective standardized tests to measure performance becomes a vehicle that increases competition between schools, between teachers, between principals. Just as failing in the market causes firms to go out of business, failing in the high-stakes testing game causes schools to close, causes teachers and principals to lose their jobs. One of the consequences of Reagan-era reforms was that state and local governments often found themselves having to meet federal dictates without receiving significant levels of federal funding. We see that with NCLB, as schools and local school districts did not have the resources to do much of what they were expected to.

With Obama's election in 2008, the thought was that NCLB would be dissolved, given the support Obama received from teachers unions. But Obama appointed Arne Duncan as Secretary of Education. Before being Secretary of Education, Duncan was the CEO of Chicago Public Schools. Throughout his tenure in Chicago, he supported the development of charter schools and the increasing marketization of education. After becoming Secretary of Education, he touted the values of mayoral takeover over locally elected school boards, and helped develop Race To The Top (RTTT), the federal educational policy that replaced NCLB. The central idea embedded in RTTT is that state educational systems, local school districts, local schools, teachers, administrators, and parents, all perform better when they compete against one another. Taking a similar approach to education systems that Bill Clinton took to cities, RTTT allocated $4.35 billion for a national competition between states. Participating states would be scored on a range of criteria, from prioritizing STEM (science, technology, engineering, mathematics) in state education programs (15 points maximum), developing and applying common standards (40 points maximum), *to creating the conditions necessary for charter schools and other "innovative" schools to thrive* (40 points maximum).

Just as in Clinton's empowerment policy, the RTTT program incentivizes market behavior and, in this specific case, further incentivizes the development of market-oriented approaches to public education. Only the states with the highest scores received funding. On paper, RTTT "rewards innovation" by giving resources to states, school systems, and teachers that increase student achievement and school quality. But by "rewarding innovation" through mechanisms of competition, the policy ended up punishing poorly performing school systems and teaching staffs, and in doing so created perverse incentives for cheating—35 Atlanta educators, including the superintendent, accused of running a sophisticated assessment-test cheating ring were indicted in 2013 for charges of theft and racketeering, and Atlanta's school system isn't alone (Strauss 2013a). Further, by requiring that failing schools either close or be privatized, the policy increasingly destabilizes public education without increasing educational quality. It bears stating at this point that charter schools perform no better and often much worse than regular public schools in educational outcomes. Furthermore, because they are far less regulated than their regular public school counterparts, poorly functioning charter schools are often allowed to continue to fail parents far longer than true "market" circumstances would dictate.[4] Finally, these legislative changes further enable a new wave of state takeovers, often managed by people who have either been trained by the institutions developed by the venture philanthropists, are TFA alum, or have been influenced by the general idea that schools work best when they function like businesses. And inasmuch as schools don't work best when they function like businesses, the various school failures that end up coming as a result only lead in more neoliberal change.

African Americans are not only particularly affected by these changes, the neoliberalization of education doesn't come without African Americans. The first vouchers and charter schools

---

4   My home state of Michigan does perhaps the poorest job of regulating charter schools. A year-long investigation conducted by the Detroit Free Press in 2014 found that charter schools spent over $1 billion per year of state taxpayer dollars with little to no transparency, with no real substantial educational progress, with very little regulation, and with significant levels of corruption (Dixon et al. 2014).

arguably appear in response to *Brown v. Board* when white Southerners decide they don't wish to send their children to integrated schools. Similarly, the spread of magnet schools — a seventies innovation — arguably comes as a result of the various rulings that enable segregated school systems to continue to exist. The connection between the economy and education that educators make in the report "A Nation at Risk" is in part a response to attempts to radicalize education often conducted by black parents on behalf of black children (Ravitch 2003). Finally, the various takeovers that radically reduce the ability of parents to make political decisions about their schools are arguably made easier when whites in general believe the (black) populations mostly affected do not have the capacity to govern themselves.

However, blacks are not only victimized by the transformations in urban education. Black elites are partially responsible for the transformations. More specifically, black political officials have often assisted in the takeover moves and have reproduced language blaming black parents and school children for poor educational outcomes. Blacks have often created public schools and managed failing school systems, and black intellectuals have themselves touted neoliberal solutions. Below I focus on a few different instances, showing how the cities I examined in chapter 2 and others like them have transformed their schools using some of the same techniques used to transform their cities. Second, I take the case of Roland Fryer—perhaps the country's most influential black public intellectual—to return to the powerful role economic theory plays in the turn.

The first wave of school takeovers began in the early nineties. In Pennsylvania in 1998, in partial response to claims that Pennsylvania schools were funded poorly by the state because it was a majority black school district, the (Republican-run) state legislature passed Act 46 and then in 2001 passed Act 83. Act 46 gave Philadelphia's Secretary of Education the ability to declare a school district in "distress", and then the ability to replace the (elected) school board of "first class" members of "distressed" districts (districts with at least 1 million persons) with a five-person "School Reform Commission" (with the governor appointing four of those individuals). Act 83 added to Act 46 by giving the Governor sole authority for removing the members of the School Reform Commission and by making teacher strikes in "distressed districts" illegal, severely reducing their ability to contest the proposed reforms. Teachers unions in such districts couldn't, for example, bargain over third-party contracts, over the provision of educational services, over class size, over staff reductions, and over the academic calendar, among other things. Furthermore, if any teacher or staff person *did* engage in a strike or a strike-related activity, that individual could be punished by having his/her certification taken away.

By definition, the only school district in the state that was eligible for takeover was the School District of Philadelphia. In 2001—the same year NCLB became law—the State of Pennsylvania did just that, with the (Republican) governor citing low test-scores, crumbling schools, and severe fiscal distress. As part of the takeover plan, the school superintendent was replaced with a CEO, and seven for-profit and non-profit firms took control of 45 public elementary and middle schools, changing them into charter schools (Gill et al. 2007). (Black) mayor John Street (who helped negotiate the terms of the takeover) was given the ability to appoint two members to the School Reform Commission. Within ten years, 35 additional schools were transformed into charters, bringing the total to 80 charters containing over 50,000 Philadelphia students. By April 2012, the School Reform Commission presented a proposal generated by the Boston Consulting Group (a global management consulting firm) that would help "right-size" the school system by closing more than 40 schools, privatizing a range of school services (including safety, cafeteria services, and transportation), and splitting the district up into five mini-districts who would be run by nonprofit and for-profit firms. This proposal itself was generated by a statewide economic crisis that saw Pennsylvania Governor Tom Corbett (GOP) cut over $300 million from the Philadelphia school budget, and was exacerbated by the decision to take out the same amount in loans, which significantly increased the school system's debt burden. Due to this debt burden, in 2013 the School Reform Commission adopted what nearly everyone called a "doomsday budget", which proposed to eliminate nearly every staff person in every school (with the exception of the school principal and a small number of teachers). This, even as Governor Corbett signed legislation to build a $400 million prison (Stroud 2013).

In 1997, Michigan Governor John Engler (GOP) proposed taking over Detroit's public schools. Although at the time (black) Detroit Mayor Dennis Archer Sr. (Dem) rejected the proposal, within two years he supported it, backing what became known as Michigan Public Act 10. The act would replace the elected school board with an appointed one and the school superintendent with a school CEO. At the time, the school system still had approximately $1.2 billion left of a $1.5 billion bond passed in 1994 for the purpose of building new schools and rebuilding the school system's infrastructure. Further, the school system had moderately increasing enrollments, a $100 million surplus, and average test scores. Within five years, the surplus had been replaced with a $200 million deficit and a number of the construction projects had significant cost overruns. The state provided the district with a $210 million loan in order to deal with the debt, but the loan itself created a debt crisis. In partial response to the crisis, the (black) CEO shut down over two dozen schools and laid off over one thousand employees. Although at the time of the school takeover the size of the student population was relatively stable, after the school closures and the layoffs almost 20,000 students left the school system (Bellant 2011).

Detroit voters eventually returned some power to an elected school board, but the school board came into office facing significant structural hurdles, partially due to the additional problems brought on by the first takeover. In 2008, the State Superintendent declared that the school system faced a fiscal emergency, and at the end of 2008 Michigan's governor declared that the school system be placed under emergency financial management, appointing African American Robert Bobb as emergency financial manager. As was the case with the city takeover of 2013, the school board remained but had no political power or authority. In 1999 and in 2008, the takeovers were touted as solutions to the district's inability to educate a majority of its students and to the district's financial problems. One of Bobb's first acts was to send layoff notices to every DPS teacher on contract—all 5466 of them (recall that the emergency financial manager legislation gave the manager the power to negate and renegotiate *all* contracts). By his second year in office he'd closed thirty more schools, and proposed a plan ("Renaissance Plan 2012") to turn almost thirty percent of Detroit's schools into charters. In 2011, Bobb stepped down, leaving the city's schools in even more debt than when he entered. That same year, Michigan Governor Tom Snyder created the Education Achievement Authority, a borderless school district that would contain the worst performing schools in the state. It currently runs several Detroit schools.

Before Hurricane Katrina, the Orleans Parish School Board (OPSB) was already under severe scrutiny, as it faced severe budgetary problems as well as corruption and graft. Within a few weeks after Katrina hit, the New Orleans community of Algiers proposed to secede from the OPSB and turn its nine schools into charters. Within six weeks of Katrina, Louisiana Governor Kathleen Blanco (Dem) proposed taking over all of New Orleans's poorly performing schools. Her plan was swiftly supported by the state legislature and passed in the form of Louisiana Legislative Act 35. This act placed 107 out of 128 New Orleans public schools under the control of a state-run "Recovery School District" and transformed over one-third of those schools into charters. Before the takeover, more than 50% of the teachers in New Orleans had 11 or more years of experience; after the takeover, the OPSB fired all 7500 teachers and staff members. After the rehiring process, more than 50% of the teaching staff had less than three years of experience (Dixson 2011). Along these lines, New Orleans schools witnessed a significant reduction in teacher salaries, benefits, and worker protections. Further, although the system—like charter school systems in general—was touted as increasing the ability of parents to choose, a significant number of students were turned away from the schools of their choice. In addition to charters, vouchers were introduced into the school system that allowed parents to send their children to private schools, further increasing competition and reducing the amount of public resources spent on traditional public schools. As of the 2011–2012 school year, almost 80% of New Orleans's public school students (42,000) attended charter schools (Akers 2012; Dixson 2011; Huff 2013).

These cases are not the only ones. In 2003, the State of California took over the Oakland Unified School District (OUSD), citing a $37 million deficit. Under the state authority, OUSD removed many of its teachers, replacing them with younger teachers from Teach For America, shut down approximately half of Oakland's public schools, and privatized many non-teaching staff positions (security guards, cooks, janitors, etc.). It also paved the way for the creation of several charter schools. After political control was returned to the school board, the OUSD student population had dropped over 30% (from 55,000 to 38,000) while its charter school population increased 400% (from approximately 2000 to 8000) to the point that almost 20% of OUSD students attend charters. And while debt was ostensibly the reason why the school district was taken over, OUSD debt tripled after the state takeover, as OUSD had to take out a $100 million loan from the state (#HandsOffDewey 2014; Allen-Taylor 2009; Anonymous 2012).

I noted that before he became President Obama's Secretary of Education, Arne Duncan was the CEO of Chicago Public Schools (CPS). Chicago is in many ways the model for RTTT. Simultaneously, the number of charter schools have increased significantly from 50 in 2005 to over 100 now, with plans for another 60 over the next few years. Spending on charters has increased to over half a billion dollars in 2014 (Bacon 2013; Sirota 2014; Uetricht 2014). Under the leadership of then-Mayor Richard Daley (Dem), the Chicago Public School system closed over 100 schools between 2001 and 2012, with most of these closings occurring under Duncan's leadership. In 2013, under the leadership of Mayor Rahm Emanuel (Dem)—a former Obama staff member—the Chicago Public School system shut down over 50 public schools at one time, affecting over 16,000 students (only 125 white), a decision brought about partially due to fiscal concerns. Further in an attempt to reduce the ability of Chicago teachers to strike, city leaders supported legislation that increased both the raw number and the percentage of union voters needed to authorize a strike. Pauline

Lipman's (2011) work is crucial to understanding the neoliberalization of public education in urban school districts.

In these and other instances across the country, we see efforts to roll back traditional public school education and to roll out neoliberal education reform, often under the guise of crisis. Political leaders in city after city call for the takeover of education in order to deal with problems of fiscal mismanagement and glaring achievement gaps, using the takeover to roll out charters, to close down local neighborhood schools, and to replace unionized teachers with non-unionized ones (often provided for by Teach For America or local equivalents). In each case venture philanthropy plays a significant role. They often provide funding for cities to transition their schools to charters, they provide funding to the larger charter systems directly, and they provide funding to institutions like Teach For America. But they also provide two other sources of aid. They provide leadership. The Broad Foundation, for example, created a superintendents academy designed to develop future local, state, and national education leaders. The first three individuals placed in charge of the Oakland Unified School District were trained at the academy, as was Robert Bobb (the first emergency financial manager of Detroit Public Schools). From 2008–2011, Philadelphia's superintendent of schools was on Broad's board of directors and headed Broad's superintendents academy.

And venture philanthropists provide ideas. I've already examined the powerful role John E. Chubb's and Terry Moe's ideas played in helping to transform common-sense ideas about education. What I want to do now is to turn to the way that the work of one specific black public intellectual has been used to not only transform schools along neoliberal lines, but to transform black children.

* * *

Roland Fryer is an African American economist at Harvard University. One of the youngest people to ever receive tenure at Harvard (the youngest African American to do so), he's the recipient of a MacArthur Fellowship (the so-called "genius grant"), the Calvó-Armengol International Prize (given biannually to the most promising social scientist under 40 studying social interaction), and in 2009 was recognized by *Time* magazine as one of 2009's "*Time* 100".

It's likely that people like Cornel West and Henry Louis Gates have had their work cited far more than Fryer—indeed, both have been in the Academy for decades while Fryer is just stating out. Furthermore, Ta-Nehisi Coates and Melissa Harris-Perry are likely more visible. However, I'd argue that, particularly at the end of the first decade of the twenty-first century, more people's day-to-day lives are influenced by Fryer.

On December 8, 2008, he appeared on *The Colbert Report*. Stephen Colbert's introduction:

> My guest tonight is an economist studying whether cash incentives will inspire students to learn more. If it works, look forward to Secretary of Education Alex Trebek (Colbert 2008).

Fryer wasn't on the show selling his recent book—you can't find any of his books on the bookshelves, because he hasn't written any. Rather, he was on the show to talk about a program designed to pay poorly performing black children in urban school districts in order to jumpstart their academic performance. Fryer, like many black academics, like many civil rights leaders, like many educators, believe that the racial achievement gap is the civil rights issue of the twenty-first century. When Fryer talks a bit about what this gap means for black academic achievement, Colbert chides Fryer jokingly, noting that even though he (Colbert) doesn't know whether or not he is black (he isn't), he believes that what Fryer is saying sounds racist. But then they get to the reason Fryer's on the show, his novel solution to dealing with the gap.

> COLBERT: You came up with the idea of paying kids to learn. How does this work?
>
> FRYER: We're in three cities, Chicago, DC, and New York. So in Chicago, for example, we're taking ninth graders, because they have a dropout issue in Chicago like many other urban districts, we're losing half of our kids in urban

> centers who are not graduating from high school. So in Chicago what we're doing is paying kids for good grades, hoping to get them on a path…
>
> COLBERT: So let's say I'm a ninth grader, I pull down… an "A".
>
> FRYER: Right.
>
> COLBERT: What do I get?
>
> FRYER: Fifty dollars per class.
>
> COLBERT: Fifty bucks per class?!?
>
> FRYER: That's right.
>
> COLBERT: Per year, or like per semester, like what?
>
> FRYER: Per every five weeks.
>
> (*Crowd "oohs"*)
>
> COLBERT: That is some *long green*, my brother.
>
> FRYER: That's right… you're black now aren't you?
>
> COLBERT: You know… I just might be… because I did terribly in school and by your own logic that would make me black.
>
> (FRYER *pulls out what appears to be a $50 dollar bill*)
>
> FRYER: Well I brought something for you, just in case you ask any good questions.
>
> COLBERT: Alright, ok, let's see if I can earn that…
>
> (Colbert 2008)

The Colbert Report was so important in part because it was so bitingly satirical. Colbert then goes into the question and answer period, beginning interestingly enough with a math question that then leads into a critique.

> COLBERT: If Danny gives Johnny $10 to copy his homework, then the teacher gives Danny $50 for turning in his homework for an A, how much money does Danny have left to give to Johnny for tomorrow's homework.… the answer is, Danny has no idea because it was his *math* homework… can this… isn't there a danger that the kids… I love this, this is the free market making kids learn.
>
> (Colbert 2008)

Here, Fryer agrees with Colbert, and then, after stating that the program hadn't been going on for that long, makes a case for his approach:

> Look, this is an innovation, I'm a guy about innovation in public schools. We are failing so many kids on a day-to-day [basis] that what we really need is to try innovative strategies so that we can close the achievement gap, so this is one such strategy... (Colbert 2008)

I've emphasized the role economists play in the neoliberal turn. Scholars like the University of Chicago's Gary Becker fundamentally changed the discipline of economics — significantly expanding the range of phenomena economists study, and also changing the *way* economists study these phenomena. Once the idea of human capital becomes fundamental to the discipline, it becomes possible to study everything from how many hours a mother reads to her child, to how political officials decide which issues to focus on when running for office, to the decisions a business makes when attempting to forecast profit margins for the upcoming decade. And once it becomes possible to do that, it becomes possible for economists to problem-solve a wide range of seemingly non-economic issues.

Although Fryer was formally trained at Penn State, he is in many ways a Gary Becker student. And he's successfully taken Becker's approach to human capital and applied it to a range of issues affecting education outcomes in black communities, including the "acting white" phenomenon.[5] Fryer, like many black academics on the one hand, and the early neoliberal economists on the other, wasn't simply interested in studying

---

5   Ever since Signithia Fordham and John Ogbu (1986) argued that black kids didn't perform as well as their white counterparts partially because blacks associated academic success with "acting white", people have been focusing on the concept as one of the most important causes of the racial achievement gap. According to Fryer, we can understand the dynamic of "acting white" as a "two-stage signaling process" in which individuals get signals from the labor market on the one hand, which demands certain things for them to get good jobs, and then from their peer network on the other, which demands certain things for them to have friends. "Acting white" occurs when the black student basically makes the decision to develop his human

phenomena for the purpose of understanding them. He studied this phenomenon because he was interested in *solving* them.

Which brings us back to the initiative he talked about on *The Colbert Report*. While still a professor at Harvard, Fryer took on two initiatives. In 2007, he was hired by the New York City Schools Chancellor to become the "Chief Equality Officer" (CEO) of New York City public schools. While CEO in New York City, over 200 NYC public schools participated in a program in which teachers were given cash incentives to increase student performance. A little more than a year later, after having served in that capacity, he helped to found (and lead) the $44 million Education Innovation Laboratory (EdLabs). The purpose of the lab?

> Good decisions are based on reliable scientific evidence. EdLabs provides reliable scientific evidence to support good decisions in education in the United States, particularly the education of minority students and students living in poverty. Our ultimate goal is to close the achievement gap and put ourselves out of business. (EdLabs)

As with many of the examples I've presented, venture philanthropy plays an incredibly important role in Fryer's work. The Eli and Edythe Broad Foundation provided $6 million to help kickstart EdLabs, and provided support for much of Fryer's research in education (Denne 2005). These initiatives enabled Fryer to try a range of projects designed to measure the impact of economic incentives on educational outcomes, and test the

---

capital in a way that will be rewarded by the market ... and is then punished by his black friend network.

Fryer and his co-author do find evidence that in some school contexts black students who get high grades tend to have fewer friends. But, this finding doesn't really hold in majority black schools, and it doesn't really hold in private schools—in fact, in private schools *whites with higher grades also tend to have fewer friends than whites with lower grades.* It really only holds in one limited context, in integrated public schools with small black populations. In other words, this phenomenon doesn't occur in the vast majority of school contexts black students find themselves in.

impact of school-based innovations on school performance. In addition to giving kids money for good grades, Fryer tried a similar cellphone-based program—high performing students in participating school districts would be given cellphones and minutes with an array of apps designed to increase their academic productivity. A number of cities with large black student populations across the country rolled out versions of Fryer's incentives program, including Chicago and Washington, DC (Hernandez 2008).

In these and other instances, Fryer used neoliberal ideas about human capital and innovation in order to change the way we think about and try to solve the racial achievement gap. Further, though, Fryer used neoliberal ideas about human capital in order to change how children *themselves* behave. Fryer believes at least one of the reasons why black and poor kids are outperformed by their white and wealthier counterparts is because they aren't properly incentivized. Black and poor kids perform poorly because they don't quite see the payoff to investing in their human capital. If they *saw* the payoff, or if the payoff was made material, by, for example, direct cash payments or nice cellphones, then kids would then see the payoff and would work better.

In each case, Fryer used his training as an economist in order to measure the impact, if any, of the innovations.

His findings were weak and not novel to people who've worked in the field of education for decades. His proposed incentive structure had no effect on student outcomes in Dallas, Chicago, and New York City (Fryer Jr. 2011).[6] Similarly, the teacher incentive program generated no positive results—there were absolutely no differences between teachers who were given cash incentives to perform and teachers who were given no such incentives (Fryer Jr. [forthcoming]). He did find that making a few key modifications to public schools—increasing the school day, spending resources on tutoring, promoting excellence, among other things—increased school quality; however, again, these findings are not novel. Yet and still, the lack

---

6   Although the *Washington Post* article about the Capital Gains program I cite above notes that students *did* perform better, data from this study wasn't included in Fryer's paper.

of new and novel findings do not prompt him, or the cities he works with, to turn back to tried and true pedagogical methods. Rather, his findings, like the neoliberal turn in education itself, are used to call for *more* (neoliberal) experimentation, are used to call for *more* (neoliberal) innovation. And everywhere we see them applied, we see the education gap increase, we see support for neighborhood schools fall, and we see support for the idea that education is a public good slowly crumble.

Whether we go back to 1800 when it was illegal to teach enslaved men and women how to read, or to the earliest efforts to create public education in Reconstruction-era America, or to the Du Bois/Washington debates of the early twentieth century, or to *Brown v. Board* which helped to break the back of Jim Crow, or to the late sixties and early seventies efforts to control local school boards, education has been contested political terrain. This is no less the case now, as the neoliberal turn engenders fierce battles over the meaning of education (do we want citizens or consumers? is education nothing more than human capital development?), over various educational resources (contracts, real estate, per-pupil spending, teacher positions), and over hearts and minds of parents and students themselves. Venture philanthropists have transformed the educational terrain, significantly tilting it in a neoliberal direction, often using their expressed desire to help hard-hit communities to support their interests in changing the face of public education. It's clear that some of the black political elites, political appointees, and intellectuals involved in the turn involve themselves either because they don't see another way out, or because they believe this represents the last best hope to defeat the educational achievement gap. However, it's also clear that some do so out of self-interest. And perhaps a thin slice of these individuals do so out of a desire to gut the concept of the public. As a result, calls for better or more moral "black leadership" are not only insufficient in beating back the turn, but arguably may be counterproductive in defeating it.

5

ON AUGUST 22, 2011, THE MARTIN LUTHER KING JR. MEMORIAL opened to the public.

When the memorial opened, Cornel West wrote a scathing editorial in the *New York Times* arguing King would *not* want a memorial—he'd want a revolution. And rather than being the standard bearer for that revolution and for King's ideals, President Obama turned his back to it, to him, and to them.

> The age of Obama has fallen tragically short of fulfilling King's prophetic legacy. Instead of articulating a radical democratic vision and fighting for homeowners, workers and poor people in the form of mortgage relief, jobs and investment in education, infrastructure and housing, the administration gave us bailouts for banks, record profits for Wall Street and giant budget cuts on the backs of the vulnerable.
>
> As the talk show host Tavis Smiley and I have said in our national tour against poverty, the recent budget deal is only the latest phase of a 30-year, top-down, one-sided war against the poor and working people in the name of a morally bankrupt policy of deregulating markets, lowering taxes and cutting spending for those already socially neglected and economically abandoned. Our two main political parties, each beholden to big money, offer merely alternative versions of oligarchic rule.
>
> The absence of a King-worthy narrative to reinvigorate poor and working people has enabled right-wing populists to seize the moment with credible claims about government corruption and ridiculous claims about tax cuts' stimulating growth. This right-wing threat is

> a catastrophic response to King's four catastrophes; its
> agenda would lead to hellish conditions for most Amer-
> icans. (West 2011)

I happened to run into Dr. West at a conference the following
week, and I told him I disagreed strongly with his editorial.
West responded by referring to the West African concept of
Sankofa, symbolized by a bird turning backwards (while walk-
ing forward) to reach an egg on its back. Expressing the idea of
understanding one's history in order to properly navigate the
future, it makes so much good common sense on the surface.
Why shouldn't we use our history to go forward? If we forget
our history, aren't we condemned to repeat it?

While West's criticisms of Obama caused him to lose his
standing in black communities, he was right to be critical
of Obama. Domestically and internationally, Obama's done
much to aid and abet the neoliberal turn. However, West's
understanding of King and of that important period in American history is too narrow. And his narrow vision stifles rather
than increases the possibilities of contesting the turn. West
privileges the Civil Rights Movement's anti-democratic tendencies by focusing on King's prophetic vision than on the
movement's day-to-day organizing and policy analysis. Further, West places more importance on "speaking truth to
power" rather than on critiquing public policy and proposing
alternatives. Finally, he significantly reduces our ability to
understand the politics of the neoliberal turn by turning to the
civil rights era. West is by no means alone in this. Many of us
routinely use the Civil Rights Movement and the leadership of
that period—particularly King's leadership—as a measuring
stick. But this doesn't make the flaws above any less important.

Rhetoric played an essential role in the neoliberal turn. A
range of "experts" made rhetorical claims about the relationship between economy, government, and society, claims that
were then translated into neoliberal policies. And a number
of black elites, including President Obama, have used rhetoric
to express support for the idea that black cultural dysfunction,
rather than neoliberalism, is the central problem facing black
people.

On Father's Day 2008 he made the following comments to a predominantly black church in Chicago.

> Of all the rocks upon which we build our lives, we are reminded today that family is the most important. And we are called to recognize and honor how critical every father is to that foundation. They are teachers and coaches. They are mentors and role models. They are examples of success and the men who constantly push us toward it. But if we are honest with ourselves, we'll admit that what too many fathers also are is missing—missing from too many lives and too many homes. They have abandoned their responsibilities, acting like boys instead of men. And the foundations of our families are weaker because of it. You and I know how true this is in the African-American community. We know that more than half of all black children live in single-parent households, a number that has doubled—doubled—since we were children. We know the statistics—that children who grow up without a father are five times more likely to live in poverty and commit crime; nine times more likely to drop out of schools and twenty times more likely to end up in prison. They are more likely to have behavioral problems, or run away from home, or become teenage parents themselves. And the foundations of our community are weaker because of it. (Politico Staff 2008)

During both the primaries and the presidential campaign, Obama consistently cajoles black people to vote, urging black audiences to get their friends, neighbors, and family members to vote, including "Pookie" and "Jethro":

> If Cousin Pookie would vote, if Uncle Jethro would get off the couch and stop watching *SportsCenter* and go register some folks and go to the polls, we might have a different kind of politics. (Tilove 2008)

In the 1990 film *New Jack City*, Chris Rock plays a struggling want-to-do-right crack addict named "Pookie" who dies trying to help undercover police officers take down a drug dealer. He is the modern incarnation of a long-running racial stereotype, the young, shiftless, black male, who means well but doesn't succeed largely because he is random and trifling.[1] Here Obama uses "Pookie" to blame black men for the lack of more transformative politics. But he never really states what that politics looks or even feels like—he leaves this to the listener's imagination. Obama consistently used poor and working-class black men to make claims about black irresponsibility. He does this in front of black audiences—his Father's Day speech is delivered to a predominantly black church, and his comments about "Pookie" were typically delivered in front of black audiences as well. But like black mayors—and to be fair some black activists and civil rights leaders as well—he delivers these comments in a way that sound like common sense to African-American ears.

And this rhetoric shapes his policy responses.

On February 27, 2014, the second-to-last day of Black History Month, Christian Champagne, a senior at Chicago's Hyde Park Career Academy, stood at a White House podium flanked by over a dozen black and Latino boys when he introduced President Obama. Christian spoke of how he encountered the President through the Becoming a Man (BAM) program, a violence and dropout prevention program led by Marshaun Baker and touted by Chicago Mayor Rahm Emanuel as having done a tremendous job in reducing violence and increasing educational outcomes of young black males.

When the President takes the podium, he talks about the BAM program, about its statistical successes (participants in BAM are far less likely to be arrested and far more likely to graduate than their peers who don't participate), and about interacting with BAM participants. He went on to talk about the network that enabled him to fail and get back up over and

---

1   Another notable example is J.J. Evans, the character played by actor Jimmie Walker on the seventies television show *Good Times*. The character J.J. Evans was not originally supposed to be as buffoonish as he appeared on the show. But as a partial response to the character's popularity, show writers (with Walker's participation) increased his buffoonish character. The tension this generated caused both John Amos and Esther Rolle to leave the show (Iton 2008).

over again. And then he talks about the importance of giving every American the same types of opportunities. Finally,
he overemphasizes the importance of ensuring that resilient
young men who make good, responsible choices are rewarded.

After listing a series of policy proposals his administration
supports in order to make sure that in fact happens, he begins
to drill down on the problems faced by black and Latino men;
however, rather than simply connecting this problem to ills
people of color face, he argues that the problem is a moral and
an economic issue for the entire nation. A moral issue, as we've
all become so used to the statistics and the various cultural
depictions of black and Latino communities that reinforce
absentee fatherhood that we're now numb. An economic issue,
as the young men left out as a result of these challenges are
unable to participate in the labor force, which ends up hurting
the nation's bottom line.

He then rolls out the program.

> After months of conversation with a wide range of peo-
> ple, we've pulled together private philanthropies and
> businesses, mayors, state and local leaders, faith lead-
> ers, nonprofits, all who are committed to creating more
> pathways to success, and we're committed to building
> on what works. And we call it "My Brother's Keeper."
>
> Now, just to be clear—"My Brother's Keeper" is not
> some big, new government program. In my State of the
> Union address, I outlined the work that needs to be
> done for broad base economic growth for all Americans.
> We have the manufacturing hubs, infrastructure spend-
> ing...But what we're talking about here today with
> "My Brother's Keeper" is a more focused effort on boys
> and young men of color who are having a particularly
> tough time. And in this effort, government cannot play
> the only—or even the primary—role....Nothing keeps
> a young man out of trouble like a father who takes an
> active role in his son's life. (Obama 2014)

Obama firmly believes, even given the structural hurdles communities face as a result of the economic downturn, that culture matters. Having a father in the home is more important in

Obama's mind than all of the structural resources in the world, as a father—particularly one who spends significant time with his child—can provide a level of role modeling that no structure can. Individuals become responsible not because some government program makes them responsible. In fact, one could imagine a government responsibility program as kind of a contradiction in terms—how can someone be responsible if they are forced by the government to do so? Instead, a far more durable method of making people responsible is by making sure people are regularly exposed to responsible adults. These adults can role model correct behavior in a way that the government cannot. And although Obama notes that there are individuals who have been able to succeed without a father in the home, indeed he is one of them, these individuals are far from the norm. To the extent that government has a role to play, its role is to on the one hand reward responsibility, and on the other develop responsibility.

Crucial components of the neoliberal turn in the wake of urban disinvestment are the public-private partnerships many cities have turned to in order to coordinate and spur interest in certain types of development projects. Private firms possess the capital and the ideas, and public institutions possess the capacity to create markets and redistribute risk broadly enough so as to entice private investment as well as the bureaucratic muscle required to coordinate the development in such a way as to fulfill political requirements. Foundations, which, while not-for-profit institutions, are still private institutions as they were created with private money, possess both the ideas—think of foundations as kind of like venture capital firms and the various programs they create as their products—and the capital needed to put these ideas into practice. Furthermore, because they, like private businesses, have a vested interest in seeing what works and what does not—they don't have unlimited resources, hence they need to have some way of distinguishing "profitable" ideas from "non-profitable" ideas—they have mechanisms in place to assess the quality of the ideas they generate. Finally, as the ability of cities and local municipalities to provide social services to needy populations diminish, foundations are a lot closer to the ground than the federal government.

The president does not have the political capital required to get anything like "My Brother's Keeper" (MBK) passed by Congress. He does, however, possess the power of the bully pulpit and the power of the Executive Order, both of which can function in such a way as to create space for private interests that are already organized around a given issue, and to incentivize foundations to become involved.

So one way to read the structure of MBK is as a perfect way to combine the strengths of government (its ability to coordinate, its ability to create markets, its ability to reduce risk) with the strengths of foundations (their ability to generate ideas, their ability to translate those ideas into local solutions, their ability to test those solutions in the marketplace), in order to deal with a pressing problem (the problems of boys of color).

I've got another take.

When he says that this is not a big government program, he in effect makes it incredibly difficult for it to *become* a government program. To the extent that we could imagine a useful function for foundations, because they trade in ideas, we can imagine foundations generating powerful ideas that function well in solving a particular problem and are scalable, that is to say, can work as well at the national or subnational level as they do at the local level, and then "giving" those ideas to the state to then translate into national policy that then can be subject to mechanisms of public accountability. Private foundations here would serve as the ideational equivalent of research and development, seeding ideas for the government to use. There are still *significant* problems here, inasmuch as private dictates are used to determine what issues get taken up, and inasmuch as expertise can often be used to trump public interests here. But let's put that aside for a moment. When Obama says that he's not talking about a big government program, he's precluding even that from ever happening. In fact, if the various institutions involved or the constituencies they potentially mobilize were to come to the realization that what they need *is* a "big government program", they'd actually have to fight *Obama* before they ever even got to Congress.[2]

---

2   Michael J. Dumas (forthcoming) fleshes this out much further.

Rhetoric plays an important role in politics. It can shape how we think about political problems. It can shape how we think about political solutions. It can shape the form that institutions take once the political will is generated to create them.

Cornel West wouldn't spend so much of his time speaking to black audiences if he didn't believe speaking to them had an effect on their politics. But in relying primarily on rhetoric that emphasizes a certain type of political leadership he misses other important aspects of political action.

Jeanne Theoharis (2013) recently wrote a powerful book about Rosa Parks that demystifies her history and the history of the Montgomery Bus Boycott. I'm going to boil her work down a bit into two stories.

The first story is the story most of us know.

One day, seamstress Rosa Parks was tired. She'd spent a long hard day working and wanted nothing more than to be able to rest her feet. Sitting near the front of the bus, she was asked to move to the back by a white patron. The white patron was within his legal rights to do so because the buses in Montgomery, Alabama, were segregated. Rosa decided she didn't want to move to the back of the bus, because she was tired. So she refused.

This put the white patrons of the bus and the white bus driver in a tizzy. They promptly stopped the bus, and had Rosa Parks arrested. Afterwards, Reverend Martin Luther King Jr. decided to organize the black community to boycott Montgomery buses. The boycott was a resounding success, leading to the desegregation of the buses and inevitably leading to the death of Jim Crow. As a result of his success in Montgomery, Martin Luther King Jr. worked to create a larger movement throughout the South, one that changed history.

Note the role black leaders and black rhetoric plays here.

Although many think of Rosa Parks as the mother of the Civil Rights Movement—indeed she is both the only woman and the only non-official to ever lie in state at the nation's capital—the traditional story limits her role to being the tired seamstress who refused to give up her seat. Martin Luther King Jr.'s role in organizing and sustaining the boycott through his charismatic leadership—particularly his rhetoric—was much more important. Any differences of opinion leading up to, during, and after the boycott, were pretty much written out of the story. Indeed, this story doesn't even tell us how long the boycott *was*.

Now, every "quick" story is going to miss some details, otherwise it wouldn't be very quick. But glossing over the details here serves a particular purpose — it enhances the general idea that black progress is purely a function of the rhetoric of black (male, charismatic) leadership. The rhetoric of black (male, charismatic) leadership works instantly and courageously. The rhetoric of black (male, charismatic) leadership galvanizes the community. The rhetoric of black (male, charismatic) leadership removes doubts. The rhetoric of black (male, charismatic) leadership organizes and directs capacity.

The second story is a bit more complicated.

Rosa Parks was a longtime political organizer, trained at a center devoted to training grassroots organizers (the Highlander Center in Tennessee). Parks worked for the NAACP and was a member of the Women's Political Council, an organization of black women devoted to racial justice and gender equality. Parks made a *tactical* decision not to get up, rather than a decision born of fatigue. Parks wasn't the first woman to get arrested for refusing to give up her seat, but people felt that only Parks had the requisite class background required to get people to rally around her.

According to the first story, until Martin Luther King Jr. came along, black people had simply laid down, unwilling to fight Jim Crow racism. Martin Luther King Jr. noted as much in *Stride Toward Freedom* when he congratulated black Montgomerians for finally "waking up" — in fact, here he also explicitly shoots down the idea that Rosa Parks's action was planned as an "accusation that was totally unwarranted" (1991, p. 424). Just as Rosa Parks had no political history at all, and simply got up when she couldn't stand it anymore, blacks in Montgomery also had little political history, finally waking up after it had passed some pre-determined boiling point.

This couldn't be further from the truth.

Even at the height of Jim Crow terrorism, blacks in Montgomery and elsewhere were organizing. Through the Women's Political Council and other organizations, blacks contested

Jim Crow racism in a number of ways decades before the movement began. Indeed, the best works on the civil rights movement (Charles Payne's *I've Got the Light of Freedom* and Barbara Ransby's *Ella Baker and the Black Freedom Movement*, for example) acknowledge that black women were the backbone of the movement, not only providing labor but tactical and strategic innovations.

We think the decision to boycott was simple.

It wasn't.

35,000 blacks in Montgomery had to be contacted and organized within days. Although given current technology we could possibly reach that many people within an hour through Twitter, connecting *and* organizing all those people required a tremendous degree of coordination and negotiation.

An action like the Montgomery Bus Boycott doesn't occur without thinking about dozens of details. It also doesn't occur without dealing with the different interests black people had. The segregated transportation system did not harm all blacks in Montgomery equally. Blacks who didn't use the bus at all, for example, suffered less than blacks (primarily female domestic workers) who used the bus frequently. Segregation created a separate economy, with black-owned businesses providing many services that whites either wouldn't supply to blacks or wouldn't supply to blacks with the same degree of care they gave to whites. Montgomery had several black taxi cab companies that had to be convinced to accept far cheaper bus fares from their passengers in support of the protest. Inasmuch as the taxi cab drivers had their own families, taking cheaper fares meant they would bring less money home to take care of their own responsibilities.

Finally, segregation was often managed by a combination of black and white middlemen. Jim Crow was an incredibly violent regime. But in order to make sure the system still worked, that the school year proceeded without a hitch, that the business community could make enough profits to grow their businesses (and by extension the city), that people were able to act relatively civil to one another even given the nature of Jim Crow, people had to manage the various flare-ups that would inevitably erupt. These black people, concerned with keeping the status quo but, in the best-case scenario, keeping violence against blacks to a bare minimum, had very different ideas about how to treat what happened to Rosa Parks than others. These different interests had to be carefully navigated, taken seriously, and dealt with.

And then, once the boycott began in earnest, an array of institutions had to be created in order to manage the various aspects of it. I mentioned the taxi cabs above. Black boycott participants originally planned to give their bus fares to black taxi cabs, who would then drive the passengers to their preferred destination. The black taxi cab companies already had the infrastructure needed to communicate with potential passengers and to coordinate with drivers — they had the staff, they had the offices, they had the phones, they had the drivers. Also, they already had the mechanism to charge customers and to keep records of the moneys paid. But this plan had to be scrapped because white political officials passed laws which prevented taxi cabs from charging passengers low fares.

This forced boycott leaders to quickly improvise in response.

Over 150 individuals volunteered their cars to drive people back and forth in response, but this too had to be negotiated and organized. Here, King and the others relied on the experience of a Louisiana pastor who'd organized a similar boycott in his home town. This pastor basically created a transportation dispatch service complete with pickup stations strategically placed throughout the city.

Donations and calls began coming in from across the country. Even though there was no real coordinated fundraising effort, people from around the world donated at least $250,000, by King's estimation. Which on the surface would appear to solve a number of the problems boycott participants and organizers could face. But it also *created* problems.

> Truly the Montgomery movement had spoke to a responsive world. But while these letters brought us much-needed encouragement, they were also the source of persistent frustration for me. The MIA lacked the proper office facilities and staff, and due to the shortage of secretarial help most of the early letters had to go

unanswered. Even financial contributions were often unacknowledged. The more I thought of my inability to cope with these matters, the more disturbed I became.

My frustration was augmented by the fact that for several weeks after the protest began, people were calling me at every hour of the day and night. The phone would start ringing as early as five o'clock in the morning and seldom stopped before midnight. Sometimes it was an ex-bus rider asking me to arrange to get her to work and back home at a certain hour. Sometimes it was a driver complaining about uncooperative passengers or a passenger complaining about a temperamental driver. Sometimes a driver's car had broken down...

We came to see the necessity of having a well-staffed office to face such problems as these. At first we attempted to run it with volunteer secretarial help. But this was not sufficient. So we hired a full-time secretary to do the regular work of the association, and set up a transportation office with a secretary to work directly in that area. (King 1991, pp. 445–46)

Finally, protestors had to not only know what they were fighting against, they had to have a clear idea of what they were fighting *for*. What would victory look like? What type of policy should be put in its place? This required them to understand the exact public policies that led to the discrimination they were fighting against, as well as the exact type of policies that needed to be put in their place. This required them to educate themselves about the law and about how it worked.

The Montgomery Bus Boycott lasted for 381 days. Far longer than anyone associated with it imagined it would go. By the end of it, participants were exalted...and exhausted.

In the simpler story, folks just got tired and then decided to move. Black male charismatic leaders gave orders. Black people followed. The plans were perfect from day one. There were no conflicts of interest. Black people didn't have differences of opinion, and if they did these differences were quickly smoothed over. It reads like a fairy tale driven by prophetic rhetoric.

The more complicated story emphasizes contingency, acknowledges conflicts of interest, and recognizes the importance of institutional development, tactical innovation, and public policy change. The complicated story emphasizes the role institutions play in generating change and the role creative individuals often play in creating institutions (better yet, in sometimes creating the *need* for institutions). The boycott involved a great deal of innovation not only in using the tactic but in modifying it to fit the unique context of Montgomery. The complicated story puts much more weight on the hard work of building institutional capacity, and far less weight on the role of inspirational rhetoric and moral suasion.

By focusing purely on King's vision as opposed to that hard work, West implies that the primary thing we need today is moral suasion. And by focusing solely on King, West ignores an entire civil rights legacy, a legacy that was far more democratic, far more inclusive gender-wise, far deeper and substantive than the tendency King represented. A model of struggle embodied by women like Rosa Parks, Ella Baker, and Fannie Lou Hamer. This struggle did have rhetorical elements, but relied far less on "speaking truth to power" and far more on organizing black poor men and women to take and wield power for themselves.

Furthermore, by going back decades before the neoliberal turn, West makes it far too easy for readers to argue that the conditions we face now are not that different from the conditions that civil rights activists faced. But this is not the case. As much rhetorical common sense as it makes to suggest that what we face now is the "new Jim Crow", to borrow a phrase from Michelle Alexander's important work, the neoliberal turn is not the twenty-first century version of Jim Crow. Jim Crow systematically withheld material, social, and psychic resources from black people regardless of their class, status, or occupation, up to and including the right to vote, the right to a jury of one's peers, the right to serve on a jury, and the right to free speech. I would have no more rights under Jim Crow given my status than my unemployed uneducated black male counterpart. Under the neoliberal turn, by contrast, I can vote, I can serve on juries, I have freedom of movement, I have freedom of speech. I can walk on the same side of the street as whites without fear of reprisal. I can start a business without fear of being lynched. If a white electrician breaks a contract with me, I can sue him and conceivably win. I can do these and a wide range of other things I used to be precluded from doing solely because of my race. This isn't to say that racism is dead and gone. Far from it. It is to suggest, though, that what we do face is not similar enough to the challenges faced fifty years ago.

Freezing both King and the Civil Rights Movement demobilizes black communities by creating a historically inaccurate perfect standard, a perfect standard that they cannot possibly hope to meet, a perfect standard the people they are being compared to themselves didn't meet. Going too often to the past freezes our tactics, strategies, freezes the very language we use to articulate our problem.

King himself recognized how important institutional development was. In *Where Do We Go From Here?*, though, written years after the bus boycott, King is far more reflective and almost melancholy. He felt that as hard as the bus boycott was, neither it nor the various successful actions that followed (including the March on Washington) could compare to the hard institutional work that had to be done in order to defend and extend the gains they made.

Not long after the moment where they'd in fact won almost everything they explicitly fought for, King was incredibly critical of his own actions as well as those of other "black leaders".

> We made easy gains and we built the kind of organizations that expect easy victories, and rest upon them. It may seem curious to speak of easy victories when some have suffered and sacrificed so much. Yet in candor and self-criticism it is necessary to acknowledge that the tortuous job of organizing solidly and simultaneously in thousands of places was not a feature of our work. This is as true for the older civil rights organizations as for the newer ones. The older organizations have only acquired a mass base recently, and they still retain the flabby structures and policies that a pressureless situation made possible.

Many civil rights organizations were born as specialists in agitation and dramatic projects; they attracted massive sympathy and support; but they did not assemble and unify the support for new stages of struggle. The effect on their allies reflected their basic practices. Support waxed and waned, and people became conditioned to action in crises but inaction from day to day. We unconsciously patterned a crisis policy and program, and summoned support not for daily commitment but for explosive events alone.

Recognizing that no army can mobilize and demobilize and remain a fighting unit, we will have to build far-flung, workmanlike and experienced organizations in the future if the legislation we create and the agreements we forge are to be ably and zealously superintended. (1991, pp. 612–13)

As one of the first modern public intellectuals, West has put a great deal of weight on prophetic utterance, on the role rhetoric plays in transforming the conditions for political action. But in a time where prophetic utterance — even when used to make neoliberalism's brutal effects nakedly evident — does more to laud prophets than it does to drive people to do the hard work needed to take control of the reigns of power, perhaps we'd do ourselves a service by leaving prophets, even ones like King, and public intellectuals in the past.

6 / SOLUTIONS

ONE OF THE HARDEST SUBJECTS TO TACKLE IN WORKS SEEKING to problem-solve the neoliberal turn is the subject of "solutions". How do we stop it? How do we reverse it?

I want to revisit the idea of the neoliberal turn. What happened?

The causes of the turn lay in two related phenomena.

First, the economic shocks of the late sixties and early seventies generated an ideational crisis. Neoliberal elites stepped into this gap, providing another set of policies that would in effect kill the welfare state. Instead of policies that protected individuals from radical market swings (through government-sponsored health insurance, unemployment insurance, incomes, and family benefits), they promoted policies that exposed individuals to them. Instead of policies that gave governments control over markets, they promoted policies that used markets to control governments. Instead of policies that supported and valued labor, they promoted policies that valued owners under the guise of promoting entrepreneurial activity. These ideas basically make competition and market-oriented behavior the guiding principles of governments and the standard by which to judge individuals, populations, and institutions.

These neoliberal ideas radically change what it means to be human, as the perfect human being now becomes an entrepreneur of his own human capital, responsible for his personal development. These ideas also radically change what it means to be free — freedom is redefined as the ability to participate in the market unfettered. This transforms the citizen into a producer/consumer. Democracy, even when (in fact, some would argue, *particularly when*) it is practiced well, is often messy — it can be hard to ferret out what the public interest is and should be in a given instance. It is inefficient. It is sometimes ineffective. The neoliberal turn replaces the democratic with the free market, assuming that individuals making market-oriented rational decisions generates better decisions (and individuals) than individuals engaged in politics—voting, debating, protesting, collectively acting in the public.

The economic shocks I mention above occur at the same time people of color begin to garner political power in the United States and elsewhere. Since the turn, we've seen capital extract more productivity from labor while paying them less in wages, causing economic inequality to rise dramatically. Along these lines, we've also seen a stark division between good jobs and bad jobs, a significant rise in unemployment and underemployment, as well as the slow death of the union. Finally, we've seen a significant increase in the cost of higher education, as more and more responsibility is placed on regular citizens to take on the risk of increasing their (and their children's) human capital. Race and racism work in justifying both the turn away from progressive (and even liberal) government and the turn towards more punitive approaches. The consequences of the turn are stark for people on the wrong end of the inequality curve, and ideas about racial difference help convince citizens that those on the wrong end of the curve are somehow different (and thus deserve their fate). Different culturally. Different biologically. As the West has never truly defined "the human" as black to begin with, and as the welfare state was not created to provide care to non-white populations, syncing the neoliberal turn to a certain type of racial project was relatively straightforward.

But it isn't as if black people have just been affected by the turn. "I'm not a businessman, I'm a *business,* man." "Momma needs a house, baby needs some shoes . . . guess what I'm gonna do? Hustle. Hustle. Hustle. *Hard.*" We *are* forced to think of ourselves this way, as the welfare state withers away, as union power declines. This isn't just a matter of force, though. This is also what we increasingly *want* to do. Who doesn't want to take care of their families? Who doesn't want to be successful in life? And as it becomes increasingly harder to make ends meet, who doesn't want to be resilient? Who doesn't want to have the required discipline? Who doesn't want to take the risks necessary to become better able to take advantage of our circumstances? We turn to people like Jay Z, Ace Hood, and people like Napoleon Hill and other prominent black entrepreneurs as models, and then adopt any number of techniques to try to be more like them.

And we pick up these techniques through a variety of black institutions. Even though black churches were never quite as political as we believed them to be—the leaders of the Montgomery Bus Boycott chose Martin Luther King Jr. and Ralph Abernathy not because they were known throughout the South as being political pastors, but rather because they were young and no other pastors in Montgomery were willing to be involved in the movement—the neoliberal turn gradually changes black churches. Increasingly, through the work of pastors like Creflo Dollar, Eddie Long, and T.D. Jakes, we see the spread of a gospel that promotes material wealth and abundance *through* spiritual discipline. Note the logic at work. Perfect followers of the prosperity gospel will submit to the discipline of the Word of God, and this disciplinary practice will not only lead to spiritual rewards, it will lead to material rewards. The "perfect" or perhaps the "perfecting" human being after the turn is the individual who consistently seeks to grow and take advantage of his human capital, forever seeking to be more and more entrepreneurial. The prosperity gospel can and should be read as an attempt to make that effort a spiritual effort. The church becomes an institution designed to assist us with developing the techniques we need to become more entrepreneurial.

Simultaneous with the growth and spread of the prosperity gospel, we see the growth and spread of megachurches—huge churches with thousands of worshippers that look more like malls than traditional church structures. Although many megachurches promote some version of the prosperity gospel, not all do. However all megachurches do rely on some combination of individual giving and public-private partnerships in order to generate the resources they need to exist. The public-private partnerships churches often engage in are themselves an important component of the neoliberal turn. As the ability of local, state, and the federal government to provide social services dwindle as a result of the turn, a variety of non-profit actors attempt to step into the gap, with churches and foundations being chief among them.

Some argue that these changes come as a result of a fall from grace. Cornel West (1993), for example, writes of black people driven by the pursuit of "pleasure, property, and power" in the wake of the Civil Rights Movement. This is decidedly not the case. As my own experience with these churches suggest, black people in these spaces are deeply moral and committed. However, the very conception of what it means to be "moral" has changed, fused to an individualist program that blames individuals for their own failings. In churches colonized by the prosperity gospel, poor men and women are poor not because of structural dynamics but because they've lost touch with God. And understand that this isn't solely a top-down process—it's not that prosperity gospel churches and megachurches change individuals, although again that does occur. The churches find *themselves* measured based on their ability to be entrepreneurial, judged and assessed by potential churchgoers who choose based on their feet and by their pocketbooks. So even as pastors of prosperity gospel churches discipline and provide disciplinary tools to their churchgoers, they are disciplined. Further, churches too are "punished" for being insufficiently entrepreneurial both by individuals (who may "punish" a church by refusing to donate the right amount or by leaving it) and by institutions. As a result of the real estate crisis, a number of churches have undergone foreclosure.[1]

The only institution viewed in and by black communities as more important than the black church is the black family. The effect of the neoliberal turn on black families is *severe*. Black families forced to hustle hard are forced to be responsible for every aspect of their life while the resources required to do so in the first place are withheld from them. Even "nuclear families" with two steady "good jobs" are not immune to the stresses here, as they are required to be ever more productive and at the same time they are expected to be more and more

---

1   The church I examined in the third chapter has changed its name and moved to a local theater, likely because of financial issues.

responsible for the costs of educating their children. But the stresses placed on working class and poor families are particularly high. As a result, the number of single parent families increase significantly, to the point that black kids in working class communities don't even see marriage as an option (Jones 2006).[2] Elites seeking to solve the problems black families face consistently adopt harsh rhetoric urging them to take more

---

2   Joy Jones's *Washington Post* article "Marriage is for White People" represents a powerful example of the class dynamics going on within black families and among black women in particular.

It's also an example of the powerful effect "way back" narratives have on our contemporary politics. Ms. Jones:

> I grew up in a time when two-parent families were still the norm, in both black and white America. Then, as an adult, I saw divorce become more commonplace, then almost a rite of passage. Today it would appear that many—particularly in the black community—have dispensed with marriage altogether. (Jones 2006)

With the first sentence we're immediately transported to a time when two-parent families were "the norm" in "the black community". And then smashed against today's reality, which Jones then spends the majority of the article addressing. As of 2012, 44.8% of black men and 43.3% of black women had never been married. Compare that to 28.4% of white men and 21.8% of white women. From this Ms. Jones moves to the causes.

> Among African Americans, the desire for marriage seems to have a different trajectory for women and men. My observation is that black women in their twenties and early thirties want to marry and commit at a time when black men their age are more likely to enjoy playing the field. As the woman realizes that a good marriage may not be as possible or sustainable as she would like, her focus turns to having a baby, or possibly improving her job status, perhaps by returning to school or investing more energy in her career.
>
> As men mature, and begin to recognize the benefits of having a roost and roots (and to feel the consequences of their risky bachelor behavior), they are more willing to marry and settle down. By this time, however, many of their female peers are satisfied with the lives they have constructed and are less likely to settle for marriage to a man who doesn't bring much to the table. Indeed, he may bring too much to the table: children and their mothers from previous relationships, limited earning power, and the fallout from years of drug use, poor health care, sexual promiscuity. In other words, for the circumspect black woman, marriage may not be a business deal that offers sufficient return on investment. (Jones 2006)

Recall that in the wake of the neoliberal turn we are all increasingly expected to act in an entrepreneurial fashion, thinking of a range of everyday activities as if we were buying, selling, or producing widgets. Having to treat ourselves as entrepreneur of our own human capital, one of the things we are forced to do is consistently conduct cost-benefit analyses, measuring the long and short term costs of our behaviors.

Above, Jones traces the cost-benefit analyses of black men and women in the "marriage market". Black men postpone marriage because they believe the benefits of postponing marriage outweigh the costs. Women, on the other hand, postpone marriage because by the time it becomes possible for them the benefits of being single outweigh the costs (because the pool of potential men doesn't meet their standards). Note how Jones refers to marriage as a "business deal" that does not offer "sufficient return on investment". Note also the reference to "risky behavior". While the straightforward way to read this is to read her as talking about the various and sundry things single men do, the other way to read this is to think about the various ways investors routinely have to wrestle with, manage, and account for risk. Along these lines, she's suggesting that because black men themselves didn't properly manage their levels of risk when they were in their twenties, they've in effect *become* "risky investments" for black women.

Her argument makes a great deal of common sense. While marriage used to be normal among blacks and whites, it's no longer normal among blacks because the costs outweigh the benefits. To the extent there's a price to be paid, that price is increasingly paid by single black professional women who can no longer literally and figuratively afford the high economic and social costs of being with black men.

There's a reason why we see "black family crisis" narratives at every single point in time from the beginning of the twentieth century to now. The resources required to build and raise families are routinely withheld from black populations and from poor populations in general. Even as the expectations placed *on* those families and the individuals within them increase. Jones notes that one of the reasons she wants a husband with which to have a child is because of the relationship she had with her father. But she also notes that one of the reasons is because she's got too many contemporary examples of shared parenthood gone awry. Here I'd argue, without knocking her decision, that she does not take into account the routine ways that black parenthood — single or otherwise — is and *was* always fraught.

And given the way we've placed the burden of parenting, of marriage, and of work increasingly on individuals and families, it's clear that a number of people are being worked harder and harder, yet at the same time expected to be better parents and better spouses. The neoliberal turn creates a condition where we are increasingly expected to be responsible for ourselves, and then increasingly expected to be responsible for our families. The stress this places on families is absolutely enormous.

and more responsibility, harsh legislation designed to surveil and punish them if they do not make the "proper" choices, and increased charity and volunteerism.

Undergirding both the family and the church is the school and the idea of education, an idea that has almost always had political overtones in black communities. In the wake of the neoliberal turn, education becomes the primary vehicle by which individuals build their human capital as well as the primary vehicle used to neoliberalize local government. Legislatively, programs like George W. Bush's No Child Left Behind and Barack Obama's Race to the Top embed competition into the structure of public education, requiring schools to compete against one another for state resources. In order to standardize the competitive dynamic, administrators measure students, teachers, principals, and the schools themselves by a wide variety of metrics. Those that perform well compared to their counterparts are rewarded. Those that perform poorly are punished. Schools that consistently fail their children are closed down.

I noted the burden placed on families. Parents are expected to act as rational consumers, collecting data on schools so as to know how well schools perform. They are expected to know their children's unique skills so as to effectively maximize them—paying to put their children in high performing sports camps if they exhibit a particular athletic talent, in various academic leadership camps so as to give them the best possible chance to get into the right colleges.[3] As early as the 1950s, when blacks in the Deep South were fighting to desegregate the Jim Crow education system, neoliberal economists like Milton Friedman argued for the value of introducing choice and competition into the school system through vouchers. Decades later charter schools—public schools run by private corporations—are becoming the norm in urban public school systems nationwide even though the research definitively shows these

---

3   In 2014, Kevin Durant was named the Most Valuable Player of the National Basketball Association. In his powerful acceptance speech, he thanked a number of players and coaches, but he spent a significant portion of his speech thanking his mother, a single parent, for

schools do *not* perform better and often perform worse than regular public schools.

In thinking through the way the neoliberal turn transforms black communities and the politics that occur within them, there can be a tendency to overstate the changes that occur as a result of the turn. Just as black people have a long history of fighting for education, black people also have a long history of using education as a way to justify hierarchies within black communities. It wasn't uncommon even before the turn of the twentieth century, when racism was in some ways far more virulent than it is now, for black people to blame racism not on whites but on poor undereducated blacks (Scott 1997). When black elites consistently promote excellence as a political project, urging that black people be excellent in spite of persistent racism, they are doing what black people like them have done for well over one hundred years. There is also a tendency to understate the role of desire. Again, who doesn't want to be excellent? What child doesn't, at some level at least, want to be a high performer? In this case, the desires of black parents and black children are used to support a project that consistently requires excellent behavior in exchange for resources, even though excellent behavior is by definition rare. But even given

---

the sacrifices she continually made for him and for pushing him to become the player he is:

> You wake me up in the middle of the night in the summertimes making me run up the hill, making me do pushups, screaming at me from the sideline of my games at eight or nine years old. We wasn't supposed to be here. You made us believe. You kept us off the streets, put clothes on the back, food on the table. When you didn't eat, you made sure we ate. You went to sleep hungry. You sacrificed for us? You're the real MVP.

The entire speech is heartfelt, and a joy to see. As a longtime fan of the game I was so proud of Durant, as he's consistently played the game the way it was meant to be played and has consistently carried himself on and off the court with grace and dignity. But while I believe his mother should indeed be thought of as the MVP, I also believe that the model of motherhood she represents is not one most working-class mothers either could or even *should* aspire to, for many reasons other than the fact that the sons of most of these mothers will not be able to grow up to be smooth shooting 6'9" small forwards. However, particularly as welfare decreases, it is the model poor mothers increasingly have forced upon them.

these tendencies to overstate the changes and to understate the role of desire, there are differences. The breadth and scope of the rhetoric is new, as are the programs themselves which persistently work to generate entrepreneurial behavior and to transform institutions.

As I note above, churches and schools are consistently disciplined under the neoliberal turn, transforming themselves into institutions capable of rational market behavior. The same type of process reshapes the cities where many of these institutions are located. I wrote about the effect of the seventies economic crisis on cities. Unemployment skyrocketed, and the demand for social services increased, but as a result of corporate and white middle-class flight (made possible by racist housing policy), revenues decreased, so cities had fewer resources to deal with the demand. Rather than increase cities' ability to generate revenue, political and economic elites hamstrung them, forcing them to rely on the bond market—which made them even less able to use revenue to provide social services.

New York City was the poster child for this move—it almost went bankrupt in the seventies because it was both prevented from raising taxes and from participating in the bond market. In exchange for getting the ability to participate in the bond market *back*, New York City was forced to cut its budget severely and subject itself to significant fiscal oversight—its budget had to be approved by an unelected board of political officials and economic elites. Increasingly, cities are viewed as economic units designed primarily to generate profit for capital, and we see an ideational shift as a variety of terms are redefined. When Clinton gave his MLK Day speech in 1994 touting his empowerment zone initiative, he defined freedom explicitly in market terms, and implicitly argued that what makes America great is not its promise of political equality and freedom but rather its ability to grow markets and develop "underused assets". America (and urban America in particular) is not the place where people can express fundamental political liberties, but rather the place where people can develop products and services for the market and then sell those services without undue regulation.

Part of this reconstruction project involves making cities good places to do business in. If a corporation cannot purchase and develop real estate in a city without dealing with environmental regulations designed to keep residents from getting sick, then it is less likely to do so. Similarly, if a corporation cannot locate its corporate headquarters in a city without tax incentives, then it's less likely to do so. Under this logic, political leaders must create the right climate for corporate partners, a climate in which their regulative burden is incredibly low, a climate in which their tax burden is incredibly low. If they create the right climate, corporations will come and the resources they expend in the city will trickle down.

Another part of this reconstruction project involves making cities good places for "productive" people—people who are either the most likely to be able to consume the goods the corporations offer, the most likely to work for the corporation, or the most likely to generate the type of buzz the city can use to further sell itself to other corporations and potential residents ("the creative class"), and relatedly the ones least in need of certain types of public goods (public housing, food stamps, etc.). This too involves incentives—tax breaks and other incentives to make urban real estate more enticing than suburban real estate, for example—but it also involves creating a favorable labor climate as well as a sense of *security and safety*. If in enticing corporations to the city urban leaders are competing against other urban leaders, in enticing "productive" people to the city urban leaders are competing against other cities but (particularly in the case of "productive" people with families) also against suburbs.

How do they create this sense? In 1994, the same year that Bill Clinton announces his urban empowerment zone initiative, two years after Los Angeles rebels in the wake of the Rodney King verdict, James Q. Wilson and George Kelling write an article for the *Atlantic* called "Broken Windows" (1982). They make three arguments. First, they argue that the rise of violent crime in urban areas across the nation is increasing and threatens to overturn and overrun the country, with most of the crime committed by the nation's poorest (and implicitly, blackest) citizens.

Second, the concept of "choice", so important in the turn, appears. They argue that crime is not a function of poverty or unemployment, but rather a function of *choice*. Criminals are not people down on their luck forced to commit crimes because they don't have jobs or stable income. Criminals are people who choose to commit crimes. And in choosing to do so they look at opportunity costs. For example, they choose one potential victim over another potential victim based on their ability to get away with the crime safely. If one potential victim appears to be able to defend him/herself, they choose a victim less likely to be able to do so. Similarly, they choose neighborhoods in the same way, looking for signs that the neighborhood and the people within them are unable to defend themselves. Sure signs of a neighborhood unable to defend itself?

Broken windows.

Third, they argue that, given that criminals choose where and when to commit crimes, and that one of the things they look for in deciding to commit crime is the ability to get away with the crime, the best way to reduce crime is to reduce the visible signs of neighborhood decay. And this is by getting police to enforce a range of nuisance laws — for example, laws making jaywalking illegal.

Wilson acknowledged that he and his co-author weren't developing social science theory. In fact, his ideas hadn't been tested. However, this didn't prevent police departments from applying them under the general heading of "zero-tolerance policing". New York City was one of the first major cities to adopt this approach, causing the rise of stop-and-frisk policies and the aggressive enforcement of a range of minor infractions, from jaywalking to jumping over subway turnstiles. Two years after the *Atlantic* published "Broken Windows", Bill Clinton signed the Personal Responsibility Work Opportunity Reconciliation Act (PRWORA). Although the *Atlantic* published no similar article about welfare during this time, *Losing Ground* (Murray 1984), published ten years earlier, packed a similar punch, arguing that the best way to deal with poverty was by refusing benefits and forcing people to work. Again the concept of "choice" played a powerful role — people were poor and unemployed because they chose not to develop their human capital in ways that would enable them to function in the market. Giving people benefits (in the form of unearned income, food, housing, child care, etc.) they didn't work for would skew their priorities and would make them more likely to make the irrational and unproductive decisions that kept them poor. Unlike "Broken Windows", the ideas in *Losing Ground* took more than a decade to percolate upwards, but when they finally did they significantly shaped the content of PRWORA.

Along with increasing societal suffering and anxiety, these policies have a few problematic effects. First, they increase the type and degree of surveillance techniques used on black and brown citizens. As a result of zero-tolerance policing. we see an increase in the absolute presence of police officers, particularly in neighborhoods deemed to be "high crime" neighborhoods. We also see an increase in technology designed to surveil populations from afar. Here I refer to the proliferation of movement-triggered remote controlled cameras that more and more employ facial recognition (hence significantly reducing the need for humans to monitor the video feed), as well as devices used to track the movement of people on parole. I also refer to the development of information technology used by welfare case managers to identify the individual work, reproductive health, and medical history of women on welfare (and often the men they have children with).

The second problem is that both approaches generate perverse incentives. By increasing the number of police encounters that lead to infractions, it in turn increases the revenue police officers bring into the city and the revenue of police departments themselves (through search-and-seizure laws that enable police departments to keep a portion of what they seize). This generates a powerful set of incentives to police black and brown bodies that goes beyond the desire to "fight crime", an incentive that becomes particularly powerful in cities that are already resource poor because of the turn. By making the most important goal of welfare policy the reduction of welfare rolls as opposed to the reduction of poverty, welfare case workers are incentivized to remove people (particularly those who don't seem to have the requisite hustle needed to find and maintain employment) rather than help them.

Third, relating specifically to the police issue, over the past several decades American police departments have progressively patterned themselves after military units, materially, culturally, organizationally, and operationally. Materially, the amount of money police departments have spent on military weapons and vehicles skyrocketed (particularly after 9/11). Culturally, it's become normal to see police in military garb, using military-inflected language and styles. Organization-ally, police have adopted military modes of organizing. Finally, operationally, police increasingly carry out their duties with a military mindset, often seeking to use violent methods of policing first as opposed to non-violent ones (Kraska 2007). And this has often occurred with the explicit aid of the federal government.

And although the relationship between black citizens and police have always been fraught, arguably the move to secure urban space has helped generate the recent wave of anti-black police violence. On July 17, 2014, Eric Garner, a New York City resident, was murdered by two police officers. In the course of trying to break up a fight, Garner himself ended up being accosted by police officers. After telling the police officers he was tired of being accosted (as part of his hustle, Garner made money selling untaxed cigarettes—a misdemeanor—and was often harassed by the police for doing so) one of the police walked behind Garner and employed a choke hold on him. He continued to deploy the choke hold even as Garner said several times that he couldn't breathe. The entire encounter between Garner and the police was caught on video by one of Garner's friends, and the video quickly went viral. On August 9, 2014, Michael Brown, a resident of Ferguson, Missouri, (population 21,000) was murdered by Darren Wilson, a Ferguson police officer, in the middle of the street. His body was left uncovered under the hot Missouri sun for several hours, in full view of his parents and neighbors. Finally, on April 19, 2015, Freddie Gray died in a Baltimore hospital due to spinal cord injuries appar-ently received during an April 12 encounter with six members of the Baltimore City Police Department.

These encounters present stark evidence of increased harassment and surveillance. In an analysis of stop-and-frisk patterns, researchers found that between 2004 and 2012 over 3.7 million black and brown men, women, and children were stopped by NYPD (Serwer and Lee 2013). Five years after "Bro-ken Windows" was published, Baltimore City Councilperson Martin O'Malley ran on and was elected mayor of Baltimore on a zero-tolerance approach to crime. His zero-tolerance policy resulted in over 667,000 arrests between 1999–2005—in 2003 alone Baltimore police made over 110,000 arrests (Snyder and Mulako-Wangota 2015). The ACLU and the NAACP later sued the city, which led to an out-of-court settlement (Fenton 2015).

In some of these encounters we see evidence of how policing has been used as an urban revenue generator. In the city of New York, policing brings in approximately $10 million in revenue per month for stopping citizens for nuisance crimes (Gonen 2015). Ferguson is one of the poorest municipalities in St. Louis County. Its second greatest source of revenue is taxing and fines. In fact, over 21% of its revenue comes from policing. Policing citizens in Ferguson and elsewhere has not only become a mechanism of preventing or responding to crime, it has become a revenue generator. The residents of Ferguson have, on average, three outstanding warrants per household (Arch City Defenders 2014). Ferguson isn't alone here — a number of poorer, predominantly black municipalities in St. Louis County have taken the same approach. The result of this approach is not only an increased tax burden, but also political disempowerment. Ferguson's black population percentage is approximately 75%. At the time of Brown's murder, Ferguson's political officials were almost all white and Republican. Working on the assumption that blacks tend to vote Democrat, and when possible tend to vote for black candidates, this particular configuration is only possible if blacks have somehow been disfranchised. In Baltimore, we don't see police used as a revenue generator as much as we do in either Ferguson or New York City. However, the city's policing budget has exploded over the past two decades. In 1991, the city spent $37 million on parks and recreation and $165 million on policing. In 2014, the city spent approximately the same amount on parks and recreation; however, it spent almost $450 million on policing (Reutter 2015). Finally, in response to uprisings in Ferguson and Baltimore, police with military-grade weapons and body armor were deployed along with military-grade vehicles. This, even though the level of property damage and the loss of life were the smallest ever recorded in the modern period for an urban rebellion.[4]

---

4   A comparison is in order. The 1967 Detroit rebellion caused approximately $80 million in damages and 43 people lost their lives. Twenty-five years later, in the Rodney King rebellions, over $1 billion in

The growing use of social media to document and spread these instances have increased the ability of people to organize against them. In response to these and other murders like them, young activists organized protests under the hashtag #blacklivesmatter,[5] garnering international attention and support.

The neoliberal turn is far broader than what I've detailed, but what I've tried to do is give a sense of its scope. But if, to quote the eighties television cartoon G.I. Joe, "knowing is half the battle", how do we get to the other half?

First, let me state what won't quite work.

Some argue that we have to return to the values of black love and care that got us to this moment in the first place, and that we have to use this self-love to begin bearing prophetic witness. Cornel West is perhaps the most important proponent of this approach. Of mainstream scholars and journalists, he and Tavis Smiley have been the most vocal in their criticism (I say "mainstream" here because there are a whole host of black scholars and activists who have been critical of Obama and the Democratic Party *for years*), and of that mainstream group they have arguably paid the biggest cost for their criticism. Here's West, writing about the politics of conversion in *Race Matters*.

> Is there really any hope, given our shattered civil society, market-driven corporate enterprises, and white supremacism? If one begins with the threat of concrete nihilism, then one must talk about some kind of *politics of conversion*. New models of collective black leadership must promote a version of this politics. Like alcoholism and drug addiction, nihilism is a disease of the soul. It can never be completely cured, and there is always the possibility of relapse. But there is always a chance for conversion — a chance for people to believe that there is

---

damages were incurred and 53 people were killed. In Ferguson in 2014, a little over $5 million in damages were reported, and there were *no* casualties. In Baltimore in 2015, while a number of police officers were injured and some estimate over 200 arrests, there were no casualties.

5   Created by Patrisse Cullors, Alicia Garza, and Opal Tometi in the wake of George Zimmerman's 2013 acquittal for the murder of Trayvon Martin.

hope for the future and a meaning to struggle.... Nihilism is not overcome by arguments or analyses: it is tamed by love and care. Any disease of the soul must be conquered by a turning of one's soul. This turning is done through one's own affirmation of one's worth — an affirmation fueled by the concern of others. A love ethic must be at the center of a politics of conversion. (West 1993, p. 19)

Above, West compares nihilism to alcohol and drug addiction, strongly suggesting that the best way to deal with this is through a politics of therapy. One way to read the work Cornel West does in bearing witness against President Barack Obama is to read him as making a last best call for Obama to exhibit the type of moral leadership required to solve the black nihilism of the underclass. For West, Obama has ignored and arguably gone against the Kingian legacy of non-violence.

Others have made many of the same criticisms West has, implicitly promoting the idea that black leaders have abrogated their responsibility to speak for and to black people's interests, and that our biggest mission is to do this in order to rebuild black communities. To an extent West is calling for a kind of *noblesse oblige* — a dynamic whereby elites, in this case black elites, do the right thing for "the black masses" out of a sense of moral obligation and duty. It sounds remarkably like what W.E.B. Du Bois had in mind when he wrote and talked about the Talented Tenth.

But Du Bois's ideas themselves were doubly problematic — first, they were based on the notion that "the masses" were culturally backward and unable to act for themselves, and second, they were based on the notion that black elites were capable of acting morally and selflessly. Although Du Bois never recognized how problematic his first idea was, he *did* recognize how problematic the second one was, discarding the notion of a Talented Tenth (Gates and West 1996). However, even here he did not totally discard his elitism — instead of the Talented Tenth he proposed a Guiding Hundredth (determined by scientifically arranging marriages and births between the best and the brightest black people). Many borrow Du Bois's ideas about the roles elites should play in black communities without recognizing the deep flaws within them, flaws that go against the democratic impulses many claim to hold dear.

Furthermore, along similar lines, some have argued that change can occur through "speaking truth to power". West and others place a significant value on "prophetic utterance". Here I'd make two claims. The first is that while we should in general be wary of using religious metaphors in talking and writing about political struggle, we should be particularly wary about the use of prophetic language, because it places more value on powerful speech (often articulated by charismatic male figures) than on labor, and hence, privileges individuals over communities, and privileges an aristocracy (based on speech) over democracy. Although intellectual labor is incredibly valuable — as I've noted, the neoliberal turn is in many ways an ideational one, created or at the very least shaped by intellectual ideas — with the turn we've seen a strong move towards monetizing intellectual production in a way that makes "speaking truth to power" lucrative for intellectuals with some combination of prestige and the right type of institutional backing. The rise of the "black public intellectual" in the nineties also comes with a rise in the black public intellectual market, a market that often rewards "truth speakers".[6]

With the rise of the internet, some people have argued that the revolution will be "tweeted". That is to say, that Facebook, Twitter, Instagram, and the like can help connect and mobilize individuals and communities across long distances. Certainly, without the Internet, the murders of Trayvon Martin, Michael Brown, Eric Garner, and Freddie Gray (among others) would never have garnered the public attention they did, and the #blacklivesmatter movement would likely not exist. At best, though, "hashtag activism" does more to *mobilize* resources for short-term high-profile events than it does to enable the type of long-term organizing and institutional development we need to counteract the turn. And at worst it shunts valuable resources away from that long-term organizing project in order to salve the internet-enabled desire for quick solutions, and creates a new set of charismatic elite hashtag brokers.

---

6   For more on this, the work of Adolph Reed (2000) is incredibly valuable.

We see a much richer account in the work of black political scientists who argue that we need to recreate a vibrant counter-public (Cohen 2010; Dawson 2011, 2013; Harris 2012; Reed Jr. 1986b, 2000). The concept of the counterpublic takes politics seriously by taking the different material interests segments of black populations have seriously, by not privileging black leadership, by acknowledging the power of ideas (particularly, I'd add, in periods of crisis), and by similarly acknowledging the power of institutions. We don't need a conversion experience. We don't need new leaders. We don't need prophets. We don't need to go back to the sixties. Further while communication technology is important, we're not going to solve our problems through technological fixes.

What do we need? I'm going to focus on a few examples of black people acting alone and in concert with others against the turn.

In 2008, Maryland Governor Martin O'Malley proposed building a $104 million prison in Baltimore for youth charged as adults, under pressure from federal officials (who argued that youth currently incarcerated in prisons with adult inmates were being mistreated). Over the past three decades we've seen a drastic increase in the number of incarcerated men and women, and we've also seen increase in the number of children charged as adults, even though the research definitively shows that children aren't necessarily developed enough to fully understand the consequences of their actions in general (much less when their actions are deemed to be criminal). The creation of an entire building designed solely to house them would further crystallize this identity. Recognizing this, two Baltimore youth organizations—the Baltimore Algebra Project and Leaders of a Beautiful Struggle (a black youth advocacy think-tank comprised of young Baltimore Algebra Project and Baltimore Urban Debate League alumni)—organized against the move, with the help of a broad coalition of Baltimore activists. After a long struggle, they ended up turning the Maryland State Legislature against the move and Governor O'Malley eventually ended up pulling his support from the project. No one likely would have predicted this outcome given the powerful forces lined up in support of it, the population targeted by it (although in the wake of Michele Alexander's book *The New Jim Crow* it is becoming easier, it is still incredibly hard to organize on behalf of black prisoners), and the population largely responsible for organizing against it (young working class and, in some cases, high school aged black people).

Activists and philanthropists supported both the Algebra Project and the Urban Debate League for two different reasons. They wanted to increase black academic achievement. They wanted to promote non-hierarchical political activism. Many if not most attempts to reduce the racial achievement gap works from the presumption of cultural dysfunction—that black and Latino populations face unique cultural deficits that adversely affect their ability to succeed academically. The solution under these circumstances is to somehow fix the kids, or to provide them what they lack culturally, with the "fixing" usually done by some authority figure. Here, founders and members of both the Algebra Project and the Urban Debate League assumed black and Latino children already had all they culturally needed to be successful. The challenge, to the extent there was one, was a challenge of translation, how to take the skills they already possessed and apply them to learn a skill they didn't necessarily think they had the ability to master. The bus ride to school kids took everyday could potentially teach them the rudiments of algebraic theory—they literally *lived* math, they just didn't recognize it as such. Kids played the dozens against one another every day; debating for them came almost as natural as breathing—it was just about mastering the form.

Both organizations were created with political goals in mind. The Algebra Project was the mastermind of Robert Moses, an SNCC organizer who also happened to have a PhD in mathematics from Harvard University. Moses understood increasing mathematical literacy as a continuation of his sixties SNCC work, which largely consisted of increasing civic literacy (Moses and Cobb 2001). The Urban Debate League itself was funded in part by the Open Society Institute in order to explicitly create ways for youth to be more involved in politics. The explicit goal with the Algebra Project was not just to get black and Latino students to master algebra through peer-to-peer education by using the skills they already had, but also to get them to apply those organizing skills—and what they were doing was, in effect, organizing—outside of the arena of math. Similarly, the Urban Debate League taught kids *policy debate*, the form of debate which is arguably the most directly related to public policy, as every year the students debate either a domestic or an international policy issue. The two organizations, as well as Leaders of a Beautiful Struggle, combined the mastery of political speech required to pointedly shoot down the various policy-driven arguments supporting the jail, arguments that often reflected a neoliberal cost-benefit analysis, with grassroots mobilizing necessary to organize hundreds of people against the attempt.

There are challenges here. A number of people have called for youth-related organizing. However, "youth" identities are by definition temporary—"youths" are only "youths" for a short period of time. Although the political interests black working class youth have may remain stable, these interests may not translate into the same suite of actions and ideas once these youth reach adulthood. There's another challenge. Youth do have the capacity to organize and the capacity to critique and develop public policy. However, their age precludes them from engaging in a wide range of activities that would have to occur in order to create sustained change over time. They cannot run for office, for example. There are certain types of contracts they cannot sign because of their age. There are hours they cannot work—during school hours or after curfew. With this said, as the people often most directly affected by policy shifts, these organizations are invaluable in increasing the ability of people to govern.

In 1988, black radical nationalist Chokwe Lumumba moved from his longtime home in Detroit, Michigan, to Jackson, Mississippi. Lumumba had been a member of the Black United Front and the Republic of New Afrika, and helped to found the Malcolm X Grassroots Movement. In 2009, Lumumba successfully ran for city council, and four years later was elected mayor. There are a few things that made Lumumba's election unique. The Malcolm X Grassroots Movement that helped elect him was a real flesh-and-blood organization, as opposed to organizations like the National Action Network or Rainbow Push (both of which function as appendages of Rev. Jesse Jackson and Al Sharpton respectively). It is relatively self-organized and has both the autonomy to organize around issues that matter to them and the capacity to work with Jackson's black communities to devise a needs-based political platform. While the organization is still a radical one, as it calls for black autonomy and for restructuring Jackson's economy, unlike many seventies-era organizations that rose and fell, it is deeply invested in seizing power through government. Lumumba was elected on the basis of the organization's ability to mobilize voters as part of a longer term plan ("the Jackson Plan") that has three "pillars": people's assemblies, electing a suite of progressive candidates, and developing a "solidarity economy".

The first two pillars work together. The People's Assembly is an institution designed to develop people's capacity to govern and make decisions, to assess the needs and wants of various sectors of the community, and to hold elected officials accountable from a place outside of the state. The progressive officials will come from and be accountable to the People's Assembly. The officials will work to implement the solidarity economy, to stave off the rise of the prison industrial complex (neutering when possible the punitive aspects of government), and reduce the power of transnational corporations to shape and direct community life. But what is the third pillar mentioned above, the solidarity economy?

> Our conception of Solidarity Economy is inspired by the Mondragon Federation of Cooperative Enterprises based in the Basque region of Spain but also draws from the best practices and experiences of the Solidarity Economy and other alternative economic initiatives already in motion in Latin America and the United States. We are working to make these practices and experiences relevant in Jackson and to make greater links with existing cooperative institutions in the state and the region that help broaden their reach and impact on the local and regional economy. The Solidarity Economy practices and institutions that MXGM is working to build in Jackson include:
>
> Building a network of cooperative and mutually reinforcing enterprises and institutions, specifically worker, consumer, and housing cooperatives, and community development credit unions as the foundation of our local Solidarity Economy

Building sustainable, Green (re)development and Green economy networks and enterprises, starting with a Green housing initiative

Building a network of local urban farms, regional agricultural cooperatives, and farmers markets. Drawing heavily from recent experiences in Detroit, we hope to achieve food sovereignty and combat obesity and chronic health issues in the state associated with limited access to healthy foods and unhealthy food environments

Developing local community and conservation land trusts as a primary means to begin the process of reconstructing the "Commons" in the city and region by decommodifying land and housing

Organizing to reconstruct and extend the Public Sector, particularly public finance of community development, to be pursued as a means of rebuilding the Public Sector to ensure there is adequate infrastructure to provide quality health care, accessible mass transportation, and decent, affordable public housing, etc. (Malcolm X Grassroots Movement 2014)

This plan is imperfect, and there are challenges here as well. The primary power the People's Assembly has to hold officials accountable is social power. Social power is very difficult to sustain over time, particularly as older members are replaced with newer ones. It is also very difficult for a horizontal organization like the People's Assembly—meant to share power broadly among the people as opposed to concentrated among a few individuals—to *stay* horizontal. Even non-hierarchical organizations where everyone has more or less the same degree of wealth and income end up developing hierarchies (based on the ability to speak or perform other functions the organization requires). Secondly, building a solidarity economy is difficult to do given the power bond-rating agencies exert over city operations and the various logistical challenges involved with generating a robust urban economy that relies heavily on locally produced goods. Finally, less than three months after Chokwe Lumumba was elected mayor of Jackson, he passed away. His son ran in the special election held to determine his successor, but came in second. A number of the plans Lumumba put in place are still there, but putting them all in motion without Lumumba's presence (both as mayor and as leader of the movement) are now going to be much more difficult.

The third example I turn to is the example of the Chicago Teachers Union (CTU). As I've already noted, education has been one of the primary victims of the neoliberal turn. Parents in urban school systems with the resources to send their children to private schools now routinely do so, unless they are able to win the equivalent of the lottery by getting their child accepted into magnet schools[7]. Charter schools and vouchers transform parents into education consumers and transform the school system into a school market. George W. Bush's No Child Left Behind and Barack Obama's Race to the Top have created federal mandates that force schools, principals, and teachers to compete against each other on an unequal playing field, with the losers being punished (principals and teachers removed, schools closed). And almost ten years before NCLB was passed, the Illinois state legislature began the neoliberalization process by giving the Chicago mayor full control of the Chicago public school system and by replacing the school superintendent with a school CEO, signaling a strong preference for a corporate manager as opposed to an educator.

Chicago's Mayor Rahm Emanuel (formerly Obama's Chief of Staff) took the radical step of closing over 50 schools in the Chicago Public School system, affecting over 30,000 students (90% of them poor and African American) (Democracy Now 2014). Although the reason proffered was budgetary—the school closings would save over $500 million, reducing the city's budget shortfall by 50%—the school board did not take the costs of busing kids into consideration, significantly reducing what cost savings may occur. But, perhaps more importantly, the decision comes at the same time the city decided to spend hundreds of millions on a sports stadium and has refused to

---

7   Of the six lottery chances my four children had for middle school and high school, we "won" the lottery five times. My middle son was the exception—he ended up going to the local middle school because he didn't get selected for the magnet middle school. He ended up getting selected for the magnet high school, however, which meant that I didn't have to think long and hard about what to do had he been forced to attend the local public high school.

consider raising taxes as an option. Similarly, while one of the arguments made in favor of closing schools was that there were too many schools for too few students, dozens of new charter schools are proposed to open over the next several years. Along the philosophy established by NCLB/RTTT, officials argued that the schools were low performing and that removing the children would be not only a good budgetary move but a sound educational move as well. But research suggests that the population purportedly best served by charters—poor students attending poor neighborhood schools—actually perform better when compared to their charter school counterparts (Caref et al. 2012). And contrary to the standard notions of a unified black political response, while many black parents and students railed against the move, the Chairman of the Chicago City Council's Black Caucus (Alderman Howard Brookins) supported the move (Dardick 2014).

In 2011, the Illinois state legislature passed a law increasing the school day and the school year in Chicago and rewarding successful teachers by reducing time to tenure. Both of these moves make a great deal of sense. The length of the school year and the idea of summer vacation itself are nineteenth-century holdovers that don't apply now, particularly given research suggesting summer learning gaps increase race- and class-based achievement gaps (Alexander et al. 2007). Others argue solid teaching should be rewarded as a way to both get teachers to strive to be better and to retain quality teachers. On the other hand, requiring a longer school year and a longer school day requires teachers to be compensated more for their labor. And if we assume that no one is born with a good teacher "gene", the fast-track project may end up disproportionately rewarding already resource-rich teachers. Teachers unions are usually the institutions best designed to work these issues out in order to ensure that teachers are adequately compensated for their work and to ensure that whatever hierarchies that do exist (some teachers get paid more than others, some teachers have more authority than others) are not the result of patronage ("hookups") or structural inequity.

But in addition to the changes above, the Illinois state legislature made one other change. To go on strike, the CTU had to have a 75% vote of all eligible members. This supermajority requirement severely limits the ability of the CTU to negotiate on behalf of their members, and through them on behalf of the children they educate. Supermajority votes (actions that require more than 50% vote of support) are incredibly difficult to garner in almost any circumstance, because union members have to subsume their own individual material interests to the interests of the union as a whole. This decision by the state represents yet another way by which local municipalities are disciplined to work with rather than against the neoliberal turn. Given the hurdles the CTU had to face, no one would have predicted that the teachers would be able to garner the necessary votes to strike.

In response to the school closings and to the persistent efforts of political officials to misrepresent their activities and to consistently criticize the work teachers performed, the CTU got the votes. In fact, they not only got the 75% needed, they received 90% (Uetricht 2014). Now, to a certain extent, in using this example I'm cheating a bit because the CTU isn't a black organization. Furthermore, I'm cheating a bit in that they weren't as successful as the other examples—they didn't roll back the school closings, nor did they roll back the general move to privatize the Chicago Public Schools. But the fact that they were able to overcome such significant legislative hurdles in getting 90% of the teachers to support work on behalf of better conditions and on behalf of black children bears inclusion. Particularly as it appears that members of the union had engaged in deep organizing for a ten year period, doing the hard work over time to build a broad base of support.

Finally, we have the #blacklivesmatter movement. Particularly with the cases of Michael Brown in Ferguson and Freddie Gray in Baltimore, we see the movement not only bringing attention to anti-black police brutality but winning signal victories. In Michael Brown's case, although his murderer Darren Wilson was not indicted, the Justice Department placed the Ferguson police department under investigation, revealing in its report the conspiracy they conducted against black citizens. Political officials explicitly incentivized police to increase the number of tickets they collected in anticipation of decreased income from other revenue streams. They appointed judges based on their ability to collect revenue rather than their ability to mete out justice. Furthermore, they routinely issued warrants for the failure to pay tickets and related fines, in effect criminalizing poverty, while simultaneously dismissing tickets they (and their friends/family members) themselves received. And they consistently violated the constitutional rights of black citizens. Over a three-year period, the City of Ferguson issued almost 450% more warrants than the city itself had residents (Friedersdorf 2015). Although it isn't clear at this point in time how the police department will change, the report creates the conditions to increase the odds that the department is gutted and transformed.

Unlike Ferguson, Baltimore already has black political representation. Indeed many of them have exhibited support for the neoliberal project I've been writing against. However, until voters elected Marilyn Mosby, Baltimore did not have a prosecuting attorney willing to prosecute police officers. Mosby was elected during the last election in a very contested race that saw her outspent by the (white) incumbent three-to-one. She ran on an explicit campaign of bringing justice to Baltimore's residents, but on an implicit campaign promise of dealing with police violence. Both the charges she brought against the officers and the speech she made in making the charges suggest that she was attentive to the broad calls for police accountability made by activists. Similar to Ferguson, the activist activity in Baltimore did not end with the charges.[8]

The #blacklivesmatter movement represents an attempt to contest this move and can be read as an attack against the neoliberal turn in three ways. Since the beginning of the twentieth century, some black elites have argued that the best way for blacks to attain the rights of full citizenship is to become "respectable"—that is, to adhere to and physically represent

---

8   Pre-existing infrastructure enabled the relatively quick creation of an activist coalition that had concrete short-, medium-, and long-term goals. The most important short-term goal was getting indictments for Gray's murder. The most important medium-term goal is twofold. The coalition wants the officers involved in Gray's murder convicted, and they want the repeal of the Law Enforcement Officers Bill of Rights. And over the long term, the coalition calls for more black control over the political, economic, and cultural resources in black communities. Furthermore, they've generated a set of clear steps that can lead to accomplishing these goals. For instance, in order to ensure a fair trial, the coalition is in the process of registering voters, because the jury pool will be chosen from registered voters.

the normative values espoused by the American middle class. The reconstruction project the neoliberal turn relies on takes the concept of respectability so critical to black politics over the last several decades and sutures it to notions of entrepreneurial hustle as well as to traditional family structures.

But not just any type of entrepreneurial hustle. Even when a social safety net existed, poor and working-class populations have had to engage in a range of hustles to make ends meet, from providing day care to selling untaxed cigarettes to using their cars as unlicensed taxicabs to hawking bootleg CDs, DVDs, and designer clothing. But the state and civil society usually frowns upon this type of entrepreneurial behavior because it doesn't generate tax revenue and doesn't shunt people into acceptable forms of income-generating employment.

Similarly, even though the economy makes it incredibly difficult for middle- and upper-income earners to sustain two-parent households, poor populations have either tried to establish two-parent households as the normative model towards which they strive or to create families as best they can. However, the state and civil society frowns down on these alternative family structures too. Whereas in the middle of the twentieth century activists felt they could only mobilize on behalf of people like Rosa Parks who appeared to uphold the values of respectability, the individuals #blacklivesmatter activists have mobilized on behalf of have been far from "respectable". Although Michael Brown was never charged with a crime, circumstantial evidence suggests that he had a violent encounter with a party store worker just minutes before his fateful encounter with Darren Wilson. Eric Garner was murdered by members of the NYPD while selling untaxed cigarettes—in fact, some argue that one of the reasons he could be heard telling police that he wasn't going to tolerate their treatment of him any longer was because they were shaking him down and he'd threatened to report them for doing so. Rather than ignore these cases in favor of more "respectable" ones (Tamir Rice or John Crawford, for instance) the #blacklivesmatter activists argued that how they behaved should not have any bearing on how they were treated by police.

In making anti-respectability the center of its politics, the movement also represents an attempt to fight for a uniquely black right to the city. The neoliberal turn swaps out "rights" with "privileges"—people don't have an inherent "right" to the city unless they perform the way the city and city elites need them to perform. These privileges are concentrated in the populations that either own the city or can behave entrepreneurially in a way that best serves the city. The #blacklivesmatter activists are implicitly arguing against distributing privileges based on ownership and entrepreneurship. As such, they are aggressively asserting a uniquely black right to the city.

All four examples have a few things in common.

First, all occurred at a moment where all seemed lost. While I wouldn't go as far as to suggest that these events suggest that neoliberalism is "naturally" contested—just as there is no "good teaching gene", there is no "contest neoliberalism gene"—I would say that while the neoliberal turn has significantly altered our ability to argue for public goods, it hasn't killed that ability. It still exists. It exists in institutions we have written off thinking they are no longer relevant—like teachers unions. It exists in populations we've written off because we believe they are incapable of radical political action—black youth. It exists in cities that we don't think of as having a long history of radical political struggle—like Jackson, Mississippi.

Second, all four recognized the fundamental role politics played in their struggles. The black youth organizers recognized that they had to pressure Maryland state legislators to kill the prison. The black radicals in the Malcolm X Grassroots Movement made electing Chokwe Lumumba a component of their organizing. The CTU chose to take the city head-on and to hold a series of town hall meetings designed to inform people of the ways political officials, philanthropists, and corporations are working together to neoliberalize and kill public education. The #blacklivesmatter movement recognized that politics was at the center of their struggle in Ferguson, Baltimore, and elsewhere.

All campaigns used moral language in making their arguments. In Jackson, they argued that the current way power was allocated was immoral because it largely concentrated all of the benefits into a few (predominantly white) hands. In Baltimore, they argued that putting $104 million to the goal of incarcerating youth was immoral given the lack of money being spent on youth in other areas, and later that Freddie Gray's (and before him Tyrone West's) murder was immoral. In Chicago, they argued that closing 50 schools was immoral because it severely impacted the ability of poor black parents and black students to get the same degree of learning their white counterparts had. However, they didn't rely on those arguments. They understood that seizing power (rather than speaking truth to it), that proposing new alternatives, would at some level have to involve political struggle. Morality wasn't enough. Even if we had a common definition of morality, a Christian-influenced morality for example, that sense of morality could still be interpreted in different ways based on material interest. Relying on morality can make it hard to move against the wealthy charter school proponent who sincerely believes that privatizing public schools represent the best hope for increasing positive outcomes among black children. Relying on morality can make it very difficult to argue against the political bureaucrat who says — as they did in the case of Baltimore — that the conditions of youth currently held in adult prisons is so bad that the moral choice would be to give them their own facility where they won't have to face the risks associated with being housed with adults. In deciding how we go about making our arguments and how we go about choosing our strategies and tactics, we should act morally — I do believe our politics have to be rooted in a certain sense of ethics. We should never, however, ignore the fundamental role politics plays and should play in our struggle.

Not only did they focus on politics, they all relied on political organizing. Organizing that included long discussions about political issues that mattered, but also parties and other events designed to get people working with each other and trusting one another. In general, people do not come to a common understanding of the structural dynamics of the problem they face, and to a common understanding of what the solution should be, through being exposed to a charismatic speaker, or through "loving black people", without having the space to talk about the issues in depth over a long period of time. The CTU organized for several years to be able to get a 90% vote. The infrastructure black youth in Baltimore relied upon was by definition designed to inculcate critical thinking skills as well as a sense of the way racism worked at structuring black life chances. The Malcolm X Grassroots Movement worked for years to build the critical capacity required to elect Lumumba, first to the city council, then mayor, and to put the political platform into action. There is no way to get around the fact that the type of work we have to do to rebuild a sense of the public interest is going to take a long time and has to start by building connections between people who may not think of themselves as political, who may not think of the various issues they struggle with as being the product of the neoliberal turn, who may not know what neoliberalism is. What I am referring to here is *not* the same as getting people to attend a rally or a march. I'm referring to political *organizing*—building the capacity of people to govern and make important political decisions for themselves—*not* political "mobilizing". Mobilizing people for a protest act of one kind or another may get people out to engage in a specific act, but unless combined with organizing work, will not cause those people to organize for themselves.

Third, in each case they were not only reactive, they were not only being critical of the turn and its effects, they proposed a positive alternative. Protest is not enough. Just as the neoliberal turn did not simply occur when the welfare state was removed, rather it occurred when the welfare state was removed and then replaced with a new program, we will not be able to build a sustainable constituency for a new world without articulating as clearly as possible what that new world will look like, what type of policies would result, what the benefits of those policies would be.

Fourth, while each of these instances represent responses against the neoliberal turn broadly considered, they each began locally. The Malcolm X Grassroots Movement has several chapters throughout the country and has already held one conference (planned before Lumumba's untimely passing) about the Jackson model (which itself is partially based on ideas developed in Spain) and how to export it to other cities. The movement against the proposed youth jail in Baltimore relied in part on data accumulated by the ACLU on the school-to-prison pipeline. And as I noted above the Chicago Teachers Union have begun organizing events all across the country to get people to understand how the privatization movement in education affects them.

And each of the #blacklivesmatter campaigns began with a specific local act of police brutality and used that act to organize locally. With this said, though, each case represents a local struggle people could experience directly. Mark Purcell (2006) argues that academics and activists alike run the risk of falling into the "local trap" by arguing that there is something inherently better and anti-neoliberal about organizing locally. I agree with him a little. The Civil Rights Movement represented in large part a fight against white supremacy as embedded in local and state politics — the local was not the site of empowerment but rather the site of profound *disempowerment* for black people throughout the North and the South. However, at the same time I argue that sustainable organizing is more likely to occur in response to a local issue (a local school closing, a rise in foreclosures in a local neighborhood, a jail built up the road, a local referendum) that can then be connected to other local issues and made national rather than the other way around. And again the Civil Rights Movement represents the best example of this — people weren't interested in ending Jim Crow as much as they were interested in desegregating the buses they took to work everyday, desegregating the restaurants they passed on the way to school, desegregating the schools themselves.

Fifth, they used a variety of black institutions in their struggles. The Baltimore youth all attended black public schools in Baltimore. They used the public schools to garner support for their work and to build relationships with black adults and black children. While a number of Baltimore area churches do promote the prosperity gospel, not all do. A few black churches in Baltimore became critical spaces for organizing against the jail — in fact, I ended up finding out about the movement against the jail in the first place through hearing a young progressive black nationalist Baltimore pastor speak about the movement. And they used popular culture. They used poetry, they used rap and hip-hop, they used parties, understanding that while again the national terrain for hip-hop may move with rather than against the neoliberal turn, they themselves could use it to speak to their local condition. And later they used these same institutions and spaces for their fight against police brutality. Similarly, in Jackson the Malcolm X Grassroots Movement did not operate from a clean slate. They relied on professors from nearby Jackson State University, they used connections with local churches to gain support for their activities. And the CTU was itself located in one of the most important institutions in black communities, schools.

Lastly, they all relied on the fundamental premise that black people had the capacity to be the change they wanted to see in the world. They neither believed that black people's fundamental condition was bruised and broken, nor did they believe that black people, because of the contemporary condition, didn't love each other. At the same time, though, they understood explicitly and implicitly that love was not enough. And while each organization does have a number of leaders, they have largely (though not fully) stayed away from the type of prophetic politics that have often created problematic internal hierarchies.

Again, there are significant differences between these instances. And even though each of these instances were victorious ones that helped to change the terrain of political struggle, there is still much more to be done. In the case of Baltimore, they stopped the youth jail but were not able to stop the privatization of Baltimore youth recreation centers, nor have they been able to (as of yet) redirect the $104 million to more progressive ends. Jackson elected Lumumba mayor but after his untimely passing his son ended up coming in second. Chicago teachers made substantial gains as a result of the strike but they were not able to prevent the 50 schools from being closed.

The #blacklivesmatter movement as it stands has not gone without critique. The most notable one is that even though the project has increased the range of black lives that people are willing to fight for, it still hasn't gone far enough. Although it's reasonable to assume, based on the limited data we have, that black boys and young men are victimized by police more than other populations (and to the extent the zero-tolerance technology itself generates broader forms of policing in places like schools), black boys and young men are not the sole target.

Black women have been victimized both directly and indirectly by police, as have black transgender populations. These
acts have in many instances been as violent as those perpe-
trated against their male counterparts, and they have been
videotaped as well. But they haven't garnered the same degree
of support and/or outrage. Extending the #blacklivesmatter
movement to include the lives of black women and transgender populations that are also the victims of police violence
would be more than simply a good thing.

However, there's a more systemic problem at work. The idea
behind "black lives matter" represents an opportunity to organize around and against a certain type of suffering, a uniquely
black suffering, made possible by the neoliberal turn. (It bears
repeating, this is *not* simply the "new Jim Crow" at work. The
odds that someone like me would suffer the type of horrific
death someone like Freddie Gray did is very slim.) However,
the politics of the #blacklivesmatter movement do not quite
match the phrase. Every single time the #blacklivesmatter
movement appears, it does so in the presence of either a horrific instance of black death or a startling instance of police
brutality. One could argue, given this, that the real politics of
the movement reflect the concept that (graphic) black death
matters rather than black life. This move makes a great deal of
sense — one way to think about this move is to think about the
way civil rights movement activists used nonviolence. Particularly when news cameras were present, nonviolent tactics of
protest tended to really highlight how violent and terroristic
white supremacy in the South and other places was. However,
by privileging the graphic black death, the victim shot in his
back while running away, the victim who had his back vio-
lently broken by police, it ends up ignoring the many forms of
non-graphic black death that occur not because of police violence per se, but because of economic violence. If Freddie Gray
hadn't been murdered by the police but rather experienced a
slow death due to lead poisoning, it's unlikely we'd be talking
about him right now. It'd be unlikely that Baltimore would've
had anything like an uprising.

Following up, by privileging black death, graphic black
death, we privilege certain types of tactics, strategies, and
institutions. We counter the spectacle of the murder with

the spectacle of the mass assembly, in the form of the protest march, or the spectacle of the mass disruption, in the form of the highway stoppage, or even in the form of the type of violent actvity the uprising hinted at. Actions, in other words, that are designed to transform the event into a black-and-white cata- lytic moment where people and the institutions around them feel forced to make a choice for the status quo or against it. And the organizations and institutions we call into being end up being those designed to generate these types of activities and to generate support for these activities (in order to grow the organizations and institutions themselves).

As far as solutions go, we also privilege anti-police legis- lation, and, perhaps more broadly, legislation designed to counter the school-to-prison pipeline. The political solution for #blacklivesmatter is to reduce the likelihood of a graphic sin- gular black death—a kid shot on the way to the corner store, a young man shot while holding a BB gun he may have planned on purchasing, a black couple driving a car with a tendency to backfire. The types of politics that generate change when the deaths come slow, painfully, and in aggregates, or when the issue is an entire legal framework (like the Maryland Law Enforcement Officers Bill of Rights) is a different politics. It is not solely or primarily a politics of the spectacle. Spectacle can work here in instances. It can be used to mobilize support. It can be used to increase awareness and general participation. And, sometimes in combination with other tactics, it can be used to disrupt. To generate and prolong crises. The types of crises that engendered the same type of problems that caused the neoliberal turn. Certainly in the case of Baltimore, a range of institutions and elites had no ready-to-roll-out solutions to the issues that the uprising called up.

But these aren't enough. It requires a politics attuned to the type of long-term institution building that builds the capacity of individuals to govern and devise alternatives themselves. It also requires a solution set that is more about combating the type of long term institutional violence that doesn't necessar- ily have a Trayvon Martin or a Freddie Gray at the center. The types of violence that instead might have Freddie Gray at the center not at the moment of his murder, but at the moment he was found to have lead poisoning.

I use these examples in order to argue that we aren't starting from scratch necessarily—some of the work is already being done on the ground.

I use these examples in order to show that we already have the seeds for a new institutional framework that re-roots the economy in politics and in the public interest. To show that we aren't alone, and that a number of people recognize another way of life is possible. There aren't as many of us as we'd like, but there are far more of us than we think.

BIBLIOGRAPHY

#HandsOffDewey. 2014. "6 Arguments for and against the Privatization of OUSD Land." *Hands Off Dewey,* September 10. Retrieved March 17, 2015. (http://handsoffdewey. wordpress.com/2014/09/10/6-arguments-for-and-against-the-privatization-of-ousd-land/).

Adderley, Nat, and Oscar Brown Jr. 1961. "Work Song." In *Sin & Soul . . . and then some.* LP. Sony.

Akers, Joshua M. 2012. "Separate and Unequal: The Consumption of Public Education in Post-Katrina New Orleans." *International Journal of Urban and Regional Research* 36(1):29–48.

Alex-Assensoh, Yvette, and A.B. Assensoh. 2001. "Inner-City Contexts, Church Attendance, and African-American Political Participation." *Journal of Politics* 63(3):886–901.

Alexander, Karl L., Doris R. Entwisle, and Linda Steffel Olson. 2007. "Lasting Consequences of the Summer Learning Gap." *American Sociological Review* 72(2):167–80.

Alexander, Michelle. 2010. *The New Jim Crow: Mass Incarceration in the Age of Colorblindness.* New York: New Press.

Allen-Taylor, J. Douglas. 2009. "Undercurrents: The End of OUSD State Control: A Tale of Two Legislators. Category: Columns from the Berkeley Daily Planet." *Berkeley Daily Planet,* July 9. Retrieved March 18, 2015. (http://www. berkeleydailyplanet.com/issue/2009-07-09/article/ 33300?headline=UnderCurrents-The-End-of-OUSD-State-Control-A-Tale-of-Two-Legislators--By-J.-Douglas-Allen-Taylor).

Alvaredo, Facundo, Anthony B. Atkinson, Thomas Piketty, Emmanuel Saez, and Gabriel Zucman. 2015. *The World Wealth and Income Database.* (http://www.wid.world).

Anderson, James D. 1988. *The Education of Blacks in the South, 1860–1935*. Chapel Hill: University of North Carolina Press.

Anonymous. 2012. "A (Brief) History of the State Takeover of OUSD." *Classroom Struggle*, February 5. (http://classroomstruggle.org/).

ArchCity Defenders. 2014. "ArchCity Defenders: Municipal Courts White Paper." (http://www.archcitydefenders.org/).

Arena, John. 2012. *Driven from New Orleans: How Nonprofits Betray Public Housing and Promote Privatization*. Minneapolis: University of Minnesota Press.

Associated Press. 2007. "Philly's Top Cop Wants 10k Black Men to Patrol Streets." *USA Today*, September 13. Retrieved February 17, 2014. (http://usatoday30.usatoday.com/news/nation/2007-09-13-philadelphia_N.htm).

Atlanta Blackstar Staff. 2014. "8 Black Pastors Whose Net Worth Is 200 Times Greater Than Folks in Their Local Communities." *Atlanta Blackstar*, June 16. (http://atlantablackstar.com/2014/06/26/8-black-pastors-whose-net-worth-is-200-times-greater-than-folks-in-their-local-community/).

Bacon, David. 2013. "Chicago Mayor Rahm Emanuel's War on Teachers and Children." *Truthout*, June 20. Retrieved March 20, 2015. (http://www.truth-out.org/news/item/17091-chicago-mayor-rahm-emanuels-war-on-teachers-and-children).

Ball, Jared. 2014. "The Ever Enduring Myth of Black "Buying Power" *iMWiL!* (http://imixwhatilike.org/2014/02/14/blackbuyingpowermyth/).

Baumgartner, Frank R., and Bryan D. Jones. 1993. *Agendas and Instability in American Politics*. Chicago: University of Chicago Press.

Bellant, Russ. 2011. "Robert Bobb and the Failure of Public Act 72: A Case Study." *Critical Moment*, March 8. Retrieved March 17, 2015. (https://criticalmoment.files.wordpress.com/2011/03/bobbreport.pdf).

Benedetti, Marti. 2007. "Faith-Based Development: Churches Lead Housing, Retail Projects." *Crain's Detroit Business*, August 12. (http://www.crainsdetroit.com/article/

20070812/SUB/708130307/faith-based-development-churches-lead-housing-retail-projects).

Bifulco, Robert, and Helen F Ladd. 2006. "The Impacts of Charter Schools on Student Achievement: Evidence from North Carolina." *Education* 1(1):50–90.

Black Sheep. 1994. "Autobiographical." *Non-Fiction*. CD. Universal.

Blyth, Mark. 2002. *Great Transformations: Economic Ideas and Institutional Change in the Twentieth Century*. Cambridge; New York: Cambridge University Press.

———. 2013. *Austerity: The History of a Dangerous Idea*. New York: Oxford University Press.

Boggs, James. 1970. *Racism and the Class Struggle: Further Pages from a Black Worker's Notebook*. New York: Monthly Review Press.

Bomey, Nathan. 2013. "Disastrous Kilpatrick Debt Deal Might Have Been Illegal, but City May Settle Anyway." *Detroit Free Press*, September 25.

Bound, John, and Harry J. Holzer. 1993. "Industrial Shifts, Skills Levels, and the Labor Market for White and Black Males." *Review of Economics and Statistics* 75(3):387–96.

Bradley, Bill. 2014. "Detroit Scam City: How the Red Wings Took Hockeytown for All It Had." *Deadspin*, March 3. Retrieved February 10, 2015. (http://deadspin.com/detroit-scam-city-how-the-red-wings-took-hockeytown-fo-1534228789).

Bunkley, Nick. 2008. "Detroit's Churches Pray for Bailout." *New York Times*, December 7. Retrieved February 12, 2014. (http://www.nytimes.com/2008/12/08/us/08pray.html).

Burch, Traci R. 2013. *Trading Democracy for Justice: Criminal Convictions and the Decline of Neighborhood Political Participation*. Chicago: University of Chicago Press.

Calhoun-Brown, Allison. 1996. "African American Churches and Political Mobilization: The Psychological Impact of Organizational Resources." *Journal of Politics* 58(4):935–53.

California Prison Industry Authority. 2014. "Welcome to the New Pia Online Catalog!" (http://catalog.pia.ca.gov/).

Caref, Carol, Sarah Hainds, Kurt Hilgendorf, Pavlyn Jankov, and Kevin Russell. 2012. "The Black and White of Education in Chicago's Public Schools." *Chicago Teachers Union*. (http://www.ctunet.com/quest-center/research/position-papers/privatization-the-black-white-of-education-in-chicagos-public-schools).

Chubb, John E., and Terry M. Moe. 1990. *Politics, Markets, and America's Schools*. Washington, DC: Brookings Institution.

Clear, Todd R., and Natasha A. Frost. 2013. *The Punishment Imperative: The Rise and Failure of Mass Incarceration in America*. New York: New York University Press.

Clinton, Bill. 1994. "Remarks on Empowerment Zones and Enterprise Communities - January 17, 1994." *US Government Publishing Office*. (http://www.gpo.gov/fdsys/pkg/WCPD-1994-01-24/pdf/WCPD-1994-01-24-Pg101.pdf).

Clinton, George. 1975. "Chocolate City." *Chocolate City*. LP. Casablanca.

CNN Wire Staff. 2011. "Philly Mayor: 'No Excuses' for Flash Mob Attacks." *CNN*, August 9. Retrieved February 17, 2014. (http://www.cnn.com/2011/CRIME/08/09/pennsylvania.curfew/index.html).

Cohen, Cathy J. 1999. *The Boundaries of Blackness: AIDS and the Breakdown of Black Politics*. Chicago: University of Chicago Press.

———. 2010. *Democracy Remixed: Black Youth and the Future of American Politics*. New York: Oxford University Press.

Cohen, Rachel M. 2015. "The True Cost of Teach for America's Impact on Urban Schools." *The American Prospect*, January 5. Retrieved March 10, 2015. (http://prospect.org/article/true-cost-teach-americas-impact-urban-schools).

Colbert, Stephen. 2008. "Roland Fryer." *The Colbert Report*, December 1. Retrieved March 1, 2015. (http://thecolbertreport.cc.com/videos/7058uf/roland-fryer).

Conlan, Timothy J. 1998. *From New Federalism to Devolution: Twenty-Five Years of Intergovernmental Reform*. Washington, DC: Brookings Institution Press.

Conley, Dalton. 1999. *Being Black, Living in the Red: Race, Wealth, and Social Policy in America*. Berkeley: University of California Press.

Dardick, Hal. 2014. "Emanuel Charter School Critics Still Not Pleased." *Chicago Tribune*, January 23.

Darling-Hammond, Linda, Deborah J. Holtzman, Su Jin Gatlin, and Julian Vasquez Heilig. 2005. "Does Teacher Preparation Matter? Evidence About Teacher Certification, Teach for America, and Teacher Effectiveness." *Education Policy Analysis Archives* 13. (http://dx.doi.org/10.14507/epaa.v13n42.2005).

Davis, Paulina, Randi Levine, and Sarah Part. 2015. "Civil Rights Suspended: An Analysis of New York City Charter School Discipline Policies." *Advocates for Children of New York*. (http://www.advocatesforchildren.org/node/852).

Dawson, Michael C. 2011. *Not in Our Lifetimes: The Future of Black Politics*. Chicago: University of Chicago Press.

———. 2013. *Blacks in and out of the Left*. Cambridge, MA: Harvard University Press.

Democracy Now. 2013. "Chicago to Shutter 50 Public Schools: Is Historic Mass Closure an Experiment in Privatization?" *Democracy Now*, May 28. (http://www.democracynow.org/2013/5/28/chicago_to_shutter_50_public_schools).

Denne, Karen. 2008. "New Education R&D Lab Aims to Advance Innovations in Public Education." The Broad Foundation. (http://www.broadfoundation.org).

Dillard, Angela Denise. 1995. *From the Reverend Charles A. Hill to the Reverend Albert B. Cleage, Jr.: Change and Continuity in the Patterns of Civil Rights Mobilizations in Detroit, 1935–1967*. PhD dissertation, University of Michigan.

Dixon, Jennifer, Lori Higgins, David Jesse, Kristi Tanner, and Ritu Sehgal. 2014. "State of Charter Schools: How Michigan Spends $1 Billion but Fails to Hold Schools Accountable." *Detroit Free Press*, July 16. Retrieved March 15, 2015. (http://archive.freep.com/interactive/article/20141030/NEWS06/310300006State-charter-schools-How-Michigan-spends-1-billion-fails-hold-schools-accountable).

Dixson, Adrienne. 2011. "Whose Choice? A Critical Race Perspective on Charter Schools." In *The Neoliberal Deluge: Hurricane Katrina, Late Capitalism, and the Remaking of New Orleans*, edited by C. Johnson. Minneapolis: University of Minnesota Press.

Dollar, Creflo. 2000. *No More Debt! God's Strategy for Debt Cancellation*. College Park, GA: Creflo Dollar Ministries.

Dumas, Michael J. Forthcoming. "My Brother as 'Problem': Neoliberal Governmentality and Interventions for Black Young Men and Boys." *Journal of Educational Policy*.

Economic Policy Institute. 2012. "The State of Working America." Retrieved September 9, 2014. (http://www.stateofworkingamerica.org/chart/swa-wages-figure-4v-change-hourly-productivity/).

EdLabs. 2015. Retrieved March 1, 2015. (http://edlabs.harvard.edu/).

Feldman, Lisa, Vincent Schiraldi, and Jason Ziedenberg. 2001. "Too Little Too Late: President Clinton's Prison Legacy." *Justice Policy Institute*, February 1. (http://www.justicepolicy.org/research/2061).

Fenton, Justin. 2010. "City Approves Settlement with NAACP, ACLU in 'Mass Arrest' Case." *Baltimore Sun*, June 23.

Fordham, Signithia, and John Ogbu. 1986. "Black Students' School Success: Coping with the 'Burden of Acting White'." *Urban Review* 18(3):176–206.

Freudenburg, William R. 2009. *Catastrophe in the Making: The Engineering of Katrina and the Disasters of Tomorrow*. Washington, DC: Island Press/Shearwater Books.

Friedersdorf, Conor. 2015. "Ferguson's Conspiracy against Its Black Citizens." *Atlantic*, March 5. Retrieved June 2, 2015. (http://www.theatlantic.com/national/archive/2015/03/ferguson-as-a-criminal-conspiracy-against-its-black-residents/386887/).

Fryer Jr., Roland G. 2011. "Financial Incentives and Student Achievement: Evidence from Randomized Trials." *Quarterly Journal of Economics* 126(4):1755–98.

———. Forthcoming. "Teacher Incentives and Student Achievement: Evidence from New York City Public Schools." *Journal of Labor Economics*.

Garcia, David R. 2008. "The Impact of School Choice on Racial Segregation in Charter Schools." *Educational Policy* 22(6):805–829.

Gates, Henry Louis, and Cornel West. 1996. *The Future of the Race*. New York: Alfred A. Knopf.

Gilens, Martin. 1999. *Why Americans Hate Welfare: Race, Media, and the Politics of Antipoverty Policy*. Chicago: University of Chicago Press.

Gill, Brian, Ron Zimmer, Jolley Christman, and Suzanne Blanc. 2007. "State Takeover, School Restructuring, Private Management, and Student Achievement in Philadelphia." Santa Monica, CA: RAND Corporation.

Gilliam Jr., Franklin D., Nicholas A. Valentino, and Matthew N. Beckmann. 2002. "Where You Live and What You Watch: The Impact of Racial Proximity and Local Television News on Attitudes About Race and Crime." *Political Research Quarterly* 55(4):755–780.

Gilson, Dave. 2011. "Overworked America: 12 Charts That Will Make Your Blood Boil." *Mother Jones*, July/August.

Glaude, Eddie S. 2007. *In a Shade of Blue: Pragmatism and the Politics of Black America*. Chicago: University of Chicago Press.

Glaze, Lauren E., and Danielle Kaeble. 2014. *Correctional Populations in the United States, 2013*. Bureau of Justice Statistics. Retrieved December 4, 2015. (http://www.bjs.gov/index.cfm?ty=pbdetail&iid=5177).

Gonen, Yoav. 2015. "NYPD 'Slowdown' Costing the City $10m a Week in Revenue." *New York Post*, January 9.

Gonzalez, Juan. 2010. "Big Banks Making a Bundle on New School Construction." *New York Daily News*, May 6.

Greco, JoAnn. 2012. "Council Hears Parks & Recreation Budget Relief Plea." *Plan Philly*, April 17. Retrieved February 22, 2014. (http://planphilly.com/articles/2012/04/17/council-hears-parks-recreation-budget-relief-plea).

Guinier, Lani, and Gerald Torres. 2002. *The Miner's Canary: Enlisting Race, Resisting Power, Transforming Democracy*. Cambridge, MA: Harvard University Press.

Hanushek, Eric A., John F. Kain, Steven G. Rivkin, and Gregory F. Branch. 2007. "Charter School Quality and Parental Decision Making with School Choice." *Journal of Public Economics* 91(5):823–48.

Harris, Fredrick. 1999. *Something Within: Religion in African-American Political Activism*. New York: Oxford University Press.

———. 2012. *The Price of the Ticket*. New York: Oxford University Press.

Helms, Matt, Joe Guillen, John Gallagher, and J.C. Reindl. 2014. "9 Ways Detroit Is Changing after Bankruptcy." *Detroit Free Press*, November 9.

Hiltonsmith, Robert, and Tamara Draut. 2014. "The Great Cost Shift Continues: State Higher Education Funding after the Recession." *Demos*, March 21. (http://www.demos.org/publication/great-cost-shift-continues-state-higher-education-funding-after-recession).

Hood, Ace, and Lex Luger. 2011. "Hustle Hard." *Blood, Sweat & Tears*. CD. We The Best/Def Jam.

Huff, Alice. 2013. "Reforming the City: Neoliberal School Reform and Democratic Contestation in New Orleans." *Canadian Geographer* 57(3):311–7.

Hursh, David. 2001. "Neoliberalism and the Control of Teachers, Students, and Learning." *Cultural Logic* 4(1).

Hurwitz, Jon, and Mark Peffley. 1997. "Public Perceptions of Race and Crime: The Role of Racial Stereotypes." *American Journal of Political Science* 41(2):375–401.

Institute for Criminal Policy Research. 2015. *Japan World Prison Brief*. Retrieved December 5, 2015. (http://www.prisonstudies.org/country/japan).

Iton, Richard. 2008. *In Search of the Black Fantastic: Politics and Popular Culture in the Post-Civil Rights Era*. Oxford and New York: Oxford University Press.

Jacobs, Elizabeth, and Jacob Hacker. 2008. "The Rising Instability of American Family Incomes, 1969–2004: Evidence from the Panel Study of Income Dynamics." *Economic Policy Institute*, May 28. (http://www.epi.org/publication/bp213/).

Jilani, Zaid. 2011. "GOP Rep. Blake Farenthold Compares Unemployed Americans to Alcoholics and Drug Users." *Think Progress*, April 29. Retrieved February 6, 2014. (http://thinkprogress.org/politics/2011/04/29/161856/blake-farenthold-unemployment-drugs/).

Johnson, Cedric. 2011. *The Neoliberal Deluge: Hurricane Katrina, Late Capitalism, and the Remaking of New Orleans*. Minneapolis: University of Minnesota Press.

Jones, Joy. 2006. "Marriage Is for White People." *Washington Post*, March 26. Retrieved February 15, 2014. (http://www.washingtonpost.com/wp-dyn/content/article/2006/03/25/AR2006032500029.html).

Kaffer, Nancy. 2012. "Detroit Water Department Restructuring Plan Would Cut 1,600 Jobs; 374 Would Remain." *Crain's Detroit Business*, August 8. (http://www.crainsdetroit.com/article/20120808/FREE/120809886/detroit-water-department-restructuring-plan-would-cut-1600-jobs-374).

Kane, Thomas J., Jonah E. Rockoff, and Douglas O. Staiger. 2008. "What Does Certification Tell Us About Teacher Effectiveness? Evidence from New York City." *Economics of Education Review* 27(6):615–31.

Katznelson, Ira. 2005. *When Affirmative Action Was White: An Untold History of Racial Inequality in Twentieth-Century America*. New York: W.W. Norton.

KBMoneywise. 2013. "Moneywise Empowerment Tour—L.A." *YouTube*. (http://www.youtube.com/watch?v=Wwm69of_WKY).

Kerby, Sophia. 2013. "Borrowers of Color Need More Options to Reduce Their Student-Loan Debt." *Center for American Progress*, May 16. Retrieved January 5, 2014. (http://www.americanprogress.org/issues/race/news/2013/05/16/63533/borrowers-of-color-need-more-options-to-reduce-their-student-loan-debt/).

Kinder, Donald R., and Lynn Sanders. 1996. *Divided by Color: Racial Politics and Demcratic Ideals*. Chicago: University of Chicago Press.

King, Martin Luther, Jr. 1991. *A Testament of Hope: The Essential Writings of Martin Luther King, Jr.* Edited by James Melvin Washington. San Francisco: Harper Press.

Kingdon, John W. 1984. *Agendas, Alternatives, and Public Policies*. Boston: Little, Brown.

Kovalik, Daniel. 2013. "Death of an Adjunct." *Pittsburgh Post-Gazette*, September 18.

Kraska, Peter B. 2007. "Militarization and Policing—Its Relevance to 21st Century Police." *Policing* 1(4):501–513.

Kretchmar, Kerry, Beth Sondel, and Joseph J Ferrare. 2014. "Mapping the Terrain: Teach for America, Charter School Reform, and Corporate Sponsorship." *Journal of Education Policy* 29(6):742–59.

Krugman, Paul. 2014. "Writing Off the Unemployed." *New York Times*, February 9.

Lacireno-Paquet, Natalie, Thomas T. Holyoke, Michele Moser, and Jeffrey R. Henig. 2002. "Creaming Versus Cropping: Charter School Enrollment Practices in Response to Market Incentives." *Educational Evaluation and Policy Analysis* 24(2):145–58.

Laczko-Kerr, Ildiko, and David C. Berliner. 2002. "The Effectiveness of 'Teach for America' and Other Under-Certified Teachers." *Education Policy Analysis Archives* 10. (http://dx.doi.org/10.14507/epaa.v10n37.2002).

Laitner, Bill. 2015. "Heart and Sole: Detroiter Walks 21 Miles in Work Commute." *Detroit Free Press*, February 10.

Lefebvre, Henri. 1996. *Writings on Cities*. Translated and edited by Eleonore Kofman and Elizabeth Lebas. Cambridge, MA: Blackwell.

Lipman, Pauline. 2011. *The New Political Economy of Urban Education: Neoliberalism, Race, and the Right to the City*. New York: Routledge.

Lubienski, Christopher. 2003. "Innovation in Education Markets: Theory and Evidence on the Impact of Competition and Choice in Charter Schools." *American Educational Research Journal* 40(2):395–443.

Lurie, Stephen. 2013. "How Washington Abandoned America's Unpaid Interns." *Atlantic*, November 4. Retrieved February 9, 2014. (http://www.theatlantic.com/business/archive/2013/11/How-Washington-Abandoned-Americas-Unpaid-Interns/281125/).

Magliaro, Elaine. 2013. "Charter Schools and the Profit Motive." *JonathanTurley.org*, March 16. Retrieved March 10, 2015. (http://jonathanturley.org/2013/03/16/charter-schools-and-the-profit-motive/).

Mahler, Jonathan. 2009. "G.M., Detroit and the Fall of the Black Middle Class." *New York Times*, June 24. Retrieved February 12, 2014. (http://www.nytimes.com/2009/06/28/magazine/28detroit-t.html).

Malcolm X Grassroots Movement. 2012. "The Jackson Plan: A Struggle for Self-Determination, Participatory Democracy, and Economic Justice." (http://mxgm.org/the-jackson-plan-a-struggle-for-self-determination-participatory-democracy-and-economic-justice/).

Martin, Darnise C. 2005. *Beyond Christianity: African Americans in a New Thought Church*. New York: New York University Press.

McAdam, Doug. 1982. *Political Process and the Development of Black Insurgency, 1930–1970*. Chicago: University of Chicago Press.

McDaniel, Eric L. 2008. *Politics in the Pews: The Political Mobilization of Black Churches*. Ann Arbor: University of Michigan Press.

Meier, August, and Elliott M. Rudwick. 1979. *Black Detroit and the Rise of the UAW*. New York: Oxford University Press.

Mink, Gwendolyn. 1998. *Welfare's End*. Ithaca: Cornell University Press.

Mishel, Lawrence. 2012. "The Wedges between Productivity and Median Compensation Growth." *Economic Policy Institute*, April 26. (http://www.epi.org/publication/ib330-productivity-vs-compensation/).

Mitchell, Josh. 2013. "Who Are the Long-Term Unemployed?" *Urban Institute*, August 20. (http://www.urban.org/research/publication/who-are-long-term-unemployed).

Moe, Ronald C. 1994. "The 'Reinventing Government' Exercise: Misinterpreting the Problem, Misjudging the Consequences." *Public Administration Review* 54(2):111–22.

Murray, Charles A. 1984. *Losing Ground: American Social Policy, 1950–1980*. New York: Basic Books.

Nellis, Ashley. 2013. *Life Goes On: The Historic Rise in Life Sentences in America*. Washington, D.C.: The Sentencing Project.

O'Brien, Matthew. 2013. "The Terrifying Reality of Long Term Unemployment." *Atlantic,* April 13. Retrieved December

16, 2013. (http://www.theatlantic.com/business/archive/
2013/04/the-terrifying-reality-of-long-term-
unemployment/274957/).

Obama, Barack. 2014. "Remarks by the President on 'My
Brother's Keeper' Initiative." *White House*, February 27.
(https://www.whitehouse.gov/the-press-office/2014/02/
27/remarks-president-my-brothers-keeper-initiative).

Oliver, Melvin L., and Thomas M. Shapiro. 1995. *Black Wealth/
White Wealth: A New Perspective on Racial Inequality.*
New York: Routledge.

Oshinsky, David M. 1996. *Worse Than Slavery: Parchman Farm
and the Ordeal of Jim Crow Justice.* New York: Free Press.

Owens, Michael Leo. 2007. *God and Government in the Ghetto:
The Politics of Church-State Collaboration in Black America.* Chicago: University of Chicago Press.

PayScale Staff. 2014. "Payscale Reveals CEO to Worker Pay
Ratios." Retrieved July 15, 2014. (http://www.payscale.
com/infographics/ceo-income).

Peffley, Mark, Jon Hurwitz, and Paul M. Sniderman. 1997.
"Racial Stereotypes and Whites' Political Views of Blacks
in the Context of Welfare and Crime." *American Journal
of Political Science* 41(1):30–60.

Pierson, Paul. 1994. *Dismantling the Welfare State?: Reagan,
Thatcher, and the Politics of Retrenchment.* Cambridge,
UK and New York: Cambridge University Press.

Politico Staff. 2008. "Text of Obama's Fatherhood Speech."
Politico, June 14. Retrieved August 10, 2014. (http://www.
politico.com/news/stories/0608/11094.html).

Preston, Darrell, and Chris Christoff. 2013. "Only Wall Street
Wins in Detroit Crisis Reaping $474 Million Fee."
Bloomberg Business, March 13.

Purcell, Mark. 2006. "Urban Democracy and the Local Trap."
Urban Studies 43(11):1921–41.

Ravitch, Diane. 2003. "The Test of Time." *Education Next* 3(2).
Retrieved March 10, 2015. (http://educationnext.org/
thetestoftime/).

Reed Jr., Adolph L. 1986a. *The Jesse Jackson Phenomenon: The
Crisis of Purpose in Afro-American Politics.* New Haven:
Yale University Press.

————. 1986b. *Race, Politics, and Culture: Critical Essays on the Radicalism of the 1960s.* Westport, CT: Greenwood Press.

————. 2000. *Class Notes: Posing as Politics and Other Thoughts on the American Scene.* New York: New Press.

Reutter, Mark. 2015. "Closing Rec Centers and Slashing Youth Programs Were Root Causes of Riot, Councilman Asserts." *Baltimore Brew*, May 4. (https://www.baltimorebrew.com/2015/05/04/closing-rec-centers-and-slashing-youth-programs-were-root-causes-of-riot-councilman-asserts/).

Robinson, Kenneth. 2008. *Destroying the Root of Debt.* Pikesville: Restoring Life Ministries.

Schram, Sanford. 2000. *After Welfare: The Culture of Postindustrial Social Policy.* New York: New York University Press.

————. 2006. *Welfare Discipline: Discourse, Governance, and Globalization.* Philadelphia: Temple University Press.

Scott, Daryl Michael. 1997. *Contempt and Pity: Social Policy and the Image of the Damaged Black Psyche, 1880–1996.* Chapel Hill: University of North Carolina Press.

Scott, Janelle. 2009. "The Politics of Venture Philanthropy in Charter School Policy and Advocacy." *Educational Policy* 23(1):106–36.

Serwer, Adam, and Jaeah Lee. 2013. "Charts: Are the NYPD's Stop-and-Frisks Violating the Constitution?" *Mother Jones*, April 29. Retrieved November 17, 2015. (http://www.motherjones.com/politics/2013/04/new-york-nypd-stop-frisk-lawsuit-trial-charts).

Shober, Arnold F., Paul Manna, and John F. Witte. 2006. "Flexibility Meets Accountability: State Charter School Laws and Their Influence on the Formation of Charter Schools in the United States." *Policy Studies Journal* 34(4):563–87.

Shostak, Art. 2006. "An Unhappy 25th Anniversary: The Patco Strike in Retrospective." *New Labor Forum* 15(3):74–82.

Sirota, David. 2014. "Chicago Mayor Rahm Emanuel Cuts Schools, Pensions While Preserving Fund for Corporate Subsidies." *International Business Times*, August 5. Retrieved March 20, 2015. (http://www.ibtimes.com/chicago-mayor-rahm-emanuel-cuts-schools-pensions-while-preserving-fund-corporate-subsidies-1648754).

Smith, Suzanne E. 1999. *Dancing in the Street: Motown and the Cultural Politics of Detroit*. Cambridge, MA: Harvard University Press.

Soss, Joe, Richard C. Fording, and Sanford F. Schram. 2011. *Disciplining the Poor: Neoliberal Paternalism and the Persistent Power of Race*. Chicago: University of Chicago Press.

Snyder, Howard N. and Joseph Mulako-Wangota. "Arrest Data Analysis Tool." Bureau of Justice Statistics. Retrieved November 22, 2015. (http://www.bjs.gov).

Strauss, Valerie. 2013a. "Atlanta's Former Schools Chief Charged under Law Used against Mafia." *Washington Post*, March 30. Retrieved February 5, 2014. (http://www. washingtonpost.com/blogs/answer-sheet/wp/2013/03/ 30/atlantas-former-schools-chief-charged-under-law-used-against-mafia/).

———. 2013b. "Teach for America — America's Fastest Grow-ing Political Organization?" *Washington Post*, October 21. Retrieved March 1, 2015. (http://www.washington post.com/blogs/answer-sheet/wp/2013/10/21/teach-for-america-americas-fastest-growing-political-organization/).

Stroud, Matt. 2013. "Philadelphia Schools Closing While a New \$400 Million Prison Is under Construction: Could It Be Worse Than It Sounds?" *Forbes*, June 17. Retrieved March 23, 2015. (http://www.forbes.com/sites/mattstroud/ 2013/06/17/philadelphia-schools-closing-while-new-400-million-prison-under-construction/).

Tabb, William K. 1982. *The Long Default: New York City and the Urban Fiscal Crisis*. New York: Monthly Review Press.

Theoharis, Jeanne. 2013. *The Rebellious Life of Mrs. Rosa Parks*. Boston: Beacon Press.

Thomas, Richard Walter. 1992. *Life for Us Is What We Make It: Building Black Community in Detroit, 1915–1945*. Bloom-ington: Indiana University Press.

Thompson, Tracy. 2014. "What Does Racism Have to Do with Gridlock? In Atlanta, Everything." *Slate*, Janu-ary 31. Retrieved February 10, 2015. (http://www.slate. com/articles/news_and_politics/politics/2014/01/

atlanta_s_snow_fiasco_the_real_problem_in_the_
south_isn_t_weather_it_s_history.html).

Tilove, Jonathan. 2008. "'Pookie' Keeps Popping up in
Obama's Speeches." *Chron*, January 31. Retrieved February 1, 2014. (http://www.chron.com/life/article/Pookie-
keeps-popping-up-in-Obama-s-speeches-1788973.php).

Tucker-Worgs, Tamelyn. 2011. *The Black Megachurch: Theology,
Gender, and the Politics of Public Engagement.* Waco, TX:
Baylor University Press.

US Bureau of Labor Statistics. 2010. "National Compensation
Survey: Occupational Earnings in the United States,
2010." *US Bureau of Labor Statistics.* Retrieved August 10,
2014. (http://www.bls.gov/ncs/ncswage2010.htm).

US Department of Housing and Urban Development Office
of Policy Development and Research. 2000. "Unequal
Burden in Baltimore: Income and Racial Disparities
in Subprime Lending." *US Department of Housing and
Urban Development.* (http://www.huduser.gov/publica-
tions/pdf/baltimore.pdf).

Uetricht, Micah. 2014. *Strike for America: Chicago Teachers
against Austerity.* Brooklyn, NY: Verso Books.

Vargas, Claudia. 2014. "PICA Endorses Sale of PGW." *The Philadelphia Inquirer*, May 22.

Wacquant, Loïc. 2009. *Punishing the Poor: The Neoliberal
Government of Social Insecurity.* Durham, NC: Duke
University Press.

Waidref, Vanessa. 2008. "Reagan's National Labor Relations
Board: An Incomplete Revolution." *Georgetown Journal
on Poverty Law & Policy* 15(2):285–313.

Walton, Jonathan L. 2006. "A Cultural Analysis of the Black
Electronic Church Phenomenon." PhD dissertation,
Princeton Theological Seminary.

Weaver, Vesla M., and Amy E. Lerman. 2010. "Political Consequences of the Carceral State." *American Political
Science Review* 104(04):817–33.

West, Cornel. 2011. "Dr. King Weeps from His Grave." *The New
York Times*, August 25.

West, Kanye. 2005. "Diamonds from Sierra Leone." *Late Regis-
tration.* CD. Sony.

Wilkinson, Mike. 2009. "Nearly Half of Detroit's Workers Are Unemployed." *The Detroit News*, December 16.

Wilson, James Q., and George Kelling. 1982. "Broken Windows." *Atlantic Monthly*, March, 29–38.

Wright, Erik Olin, and Rachel Dwyer. 2000. *The American Jobs Machine*. Retrieved December 16, 2013. (http://www.ssc. wisc.edu/~wright/Job-BR.PDF).

Wright, Joshua. 2013. "Temp Employment Is Dominating Job Growth in the Largest Cities." *EMSI*, June 21. Retrieved December 20, 2013. (http://www.economicmodeling. com/2013/06/21/temp-employment-is-dominating-job-growth-in-the-largest-cities-is-that-a-good-thing/).

Zimmer, Ron, and Richard Buddin. 2006. "Charter School Performance in Two Large Urban Districts." *Journal of Urban Economics* 60(2):307–26.

CPSIA information can be obtained
at www.ICGtesting.com
Printed in the USA
LVHW080725160419
614312LV00001BA/1/P